are gorgeous boys and a credit to Ian. The whole area of needs very careful thinking through, but in Ian's case it was about him wanting children. Being a parent is a demanding anyone—he is energetic, talented, and devoted to the triplets. I was delighted to become godmother.'

Esther Rantzen, Lars' godmother.

rs was born first, then Ian, and a minute later Lars. They are renti going to nursery and are learning how to read; they will be g to school in a year and a half. Ian is currently deciding to which school they will be going.

How do we find our way to a happy and fulfilled life? While caring for his parents at home, Ian Mucklejohn wanted more than a busy working life. He deeply longed for a family but did not want to abandon his increasingly dependent parents. He had resigned himself to the fact that it would be hard to find the woman of his dreams who would want to share the demanding care for his father in particular.

It was only when a friend happened to mention parenting by surrogacy that he set out on a journey that would make his . In And Then There Were Three he tells the exceptio story of the surrogate birth of Ian's triplet sons—Lars, Ian and Piers—and what happened when someone tipped off a national newspaper. Supported by Esther Rantzen and m other well-wishers for the three boys, Ian chronicles the boys' family life throughout this turbulent period.

Writing how the boys have enriched his life and changed his outlook forever, Ian's account is a touching account of an exceptional family life.

Ian Mucklejohn is in full charge of raising his children. Ian's mother and father, both of whom he adored, both reached a very advanced age. His father recently died of dementia, not long after the boys were born.

And Then
There Were Three

GIBSON SQUARE

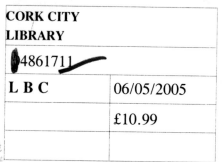

This edition published for the first time in 2005 in the UK by

Gibson Square Books Ltd
15 Gibson Square, London N1 0RD
Tel: +44 (0)20 7689 4790; Fax: +44 (0)20 7689 7395
info@gibsonsquare.com
www.gibsonsquare.com

© 2005 by Ian Mucklejohn

ISBN 1-903933-55-2

Sales by Signature
Castlegate 20, York YO1 9RP
Tel 01904 633 633; Fax 01904 675 445
sales@signaturebooks.co.uk
www.signaturebooks.co.uk

UK distribution by Central Books Ltd
99 Wallis Road, UK London E9 5LN
Tel +44 (0)845 458 9911; Fax +44 (0)845 458 9912
info@centralbooks.com
www.centralbooks.com

Printed by Bell & Bain Ltd., Glasgow

Contents

For My Parents

'My giggles. I want my giggles!'

Blue eyes welled and trickled down cheeks now puffed and puce. The crescendo of Piers's agitation silenced the party. Frankenstein-like, syringe in one hand, chain-saw in the other, stethoscope around the shoulders, hard hat perched jauntily over one eye, Ian injected and then pruned Lars's arm. Crumpled packaging trampled underfoot, the doctor's set and the builder's set had become one.

'Where's my GIGGLES!'

Intent on his goal, Piers hitched his dungarees higher, pushed the gift wrapping aside and strode forward with all the speed his three year-old legs could muster.

'My giggles,' he sobbed. 'He's got my giggles.'

Ian turned, jaw dropped, knowing he was the quarry. Piers' fingers flailed at his brother's eyes, grasping the yellow goggles strapped across them. With a pull, the elastic slipped and the prize fell into the clutching hand.

'MY giggles,' Piers informed us. 'Not Ian's.'

One of the adults came over to me to elucidate. 'My fault. I told him he looked like Biggles.'

Tears instantly evaporated, face clear and beaming, hardly able to see through the smeared lenses of his goggles, Piers continued playing happily amid the detritus through which Lars and Ian, making dee-dah noises, manoeuvred crushed boxes. Cardboard, paper, sticky tape, sophisticated electronic engineering, it was all the same to them. A toy was a toy.

Out came the cakes. One white; one chocolate; one red.

'Blow. Blow. Come on—blow!'

Lips pursed lightly with a slight exhalation upwards.

'No, not up your nose. Blow the candles out!'

As this was only the third time birthday cake candles had needed to be blown out and they could not remember the first and second, puzzlement spread across their faces. Godparents to the rescue, the nine small flames were extinguished into spirals of dark smoke. The boys looked for where the gleam of brilliance had gone.

'Cut the cakes!'

Before they could wonder any longer, they were whisked to the kitchen . Each right hand ensconced in an adult's, their tiny fingers touched the knives as the shiny coloured coverings fragmented into slivers of icing sugar revealing soft pillows of sponge and oozings of jam beneath. Fingers wriggled from adult hands to touch the sticky softness, to press it into shapes, to direct it via cheek and chin to the mouth, to gorge on the sweetness of it all.

'Right everyone,' I said, 'The Professor is putting Punch and Judy on in the sitting room.'

1

'Your Turn'

The dangling slipper led to a foot which led to a leg which led to a lap as a small child made his way along the sofa in the nursery. Already cradled in the lap was another small child. A third was eyeing his brothers' progress and crawling through the obstacle course of toys. A hand reached out and stroked the child on the lap. Through the hair and down the back the hand moved rhythmically. The child moved across onto the cushion and slid onto the carpet. Another child took the place of the first. The stroking continued. That child followed his brother. The hand, oblivious, stroked the arm of the sofa. 'Come on Piers, your turn', I said. The child looked into the grey eyes staring into the middle distance. I put him on my father's lap. He stroked Piers's blonde hair.

'Is it a baby or a cat?' I asked.

'Cat,' came the immediate reply.

My father had lived just long enough for his grandsons to call him 'Grandad'. For a small part of his long life of ninety four years, he had known for a few seconds at a time that he had grandchildren. Oblivious to reality, his was a half-world of shadows from the past—enabling him to quote verbatim from his 1918 school report ('A bright and intelligent boy; always attentive and well-behaved') and to know that he had been in 'Dwyer Ward One' with appendicitis at the age of five—while remaining unaware of the season, the year or, increasingly, who I was.

He would recite in its entirety Longfellow's 'Psalm of Life'.—'Life is real! Life is earnest! And the grave is not its goal; Dust thou art, to dust returnest, Was not spoken of the soul'—but had no idea of a name of the town he had lived in for more than fifty years. One by one his faculties were closing down. The one-time sportsman, spokesman, committee man, protector, bread-winner and beloved father had become utterly dependent and helpless.

Even in his final year, there were moments of clarity. For just a few seconds at a time the cranial connections worked. I had been chatting about the boys, concentrating on driving, providing mental stimulation as a matter of course. 'What are their names?' My eyes moved from the road ahead. I looked him full in the face.

He was staring intently at me. 'Piers, Ian and Lars.'

'Don't think much of those.'

'What do you think I should have called them?'

He considered for a moment. 'Matthew' was the reply.

'Why?'

'Don't know. I just like the name.'

'If you'd told me that a few months ago, I would

have called one of them that name, but it's a bit late now.'

'Oh.'

'I love you, father.'

'I love you, Ian.' He paused, looking me full in the face. 'Passionately.' He meant it.

'More than anything I want to tell you all about it, but you'll be switching off in a few seconds so I can't. I wish I had you back.'

The glazed look had returned. Once again I had lost my father.

Lars peered through the raised plastic canopy of his flying saucer.

'House is yellow. Bathroom's yellow. You're yellow.'

He squinted at his brother. 'You're yellow, Bruce.'

Bruce was the name of an imaginary dog at nursery school.

'How do you like being Bruce, Ian?'

'I'm Aidan. Ian Aidan and I'm a good boy, daddy.' His interrogatory look belied the confidence of his statement.

'Of course you are. Most of the time.'

In a voice half an octave too high for comfort, Lars asserted himself. 'I'm putting my motorbike on the window sill'.

He gathered red socks, green pants patterned with spiders, blue trimmed vest, beige trousers and a grey top with a red Harley-Davidson splashed across the front in one hand and Pooh Bear in the other. Climbing up a small plastic step, he pressed them onto the window sill. He held his arms open to be lifted onto the lavatory and sneezed.

'Bless you.'

'Yes,' he said—adding 'bless me.'

'Shoes or slippers?' Having arranged the clothes at the foot of each cot, Piers wanted to take out the right footwear.

Generally it was shoes on a school day, otherwise slippers. He pulled open the sliding mirrored double doors gently, avoiding the spring back as the limit of travel was reached, and slid the mesh shoe-drawer out. He placed six slippers in serried ranks and stood back to admire the symmetry. It was momentary. Ian flew from the bathroom along the cots. In his wake a colourful trail of flotsam.

'It's called 'having brothers', Piers.'

'Can I take baby?'

'Yes, Ian.'

'No, don't WANT baby. Want Muck.' A red plastic digger was pulled from the toy box, its electronic voice singing "Bob the Builder, can we fix it? Bob the Builder, yes we can".'

'No we can't,' added Lars.

2

A Natural Swing

To make his point, my father's fist banged on the table. The words were a blur, but the actions spoke for themselves. I was sitting at the dining table on that Saturday lunchtime on that winter's day in 1957 when I was ten. I had no idea what it was, but it must have been something I had done.

I had finished my rice pudding, or maybe I hadn't and that was the problem. My father had not.

He had been working himself into a rage during the whole meal because my mother was not backing him up. I wanted to leave the table. Asking to do so never occurred to me as it was accepted that my mother, father and I would finish a meal together.

My mother carried on eating. It was her way of coping. She rode it. She didn't, of course. The outburst terrified her as much as it did me.

'Calm down, John.' 'John' had been the only part of his name she had caught when they had been introduced at a cricket club in the 1930s. She had never reconciled herself to his real name being 'Herbert'.

A Natural Swing

Down and down the fist pounded. I watched trans-fixed. Everything around us was normal. The room, the furniture, the view through the French windows into the garden that was my father's joy. Past the skeletal fruit trees, up to the trellis that separated the grassed area from the vegetables.

Yet there in front of this familiarity was my father enraged as I had never seen him before. In one hand the spoon; the other hand continued its downward path. Bang, bang, bang—splodge. His fist caught the side of the bowl, sending it towards his chest down into his lap and the contents into his face which, now florid, was striated with white. At a distance of several decades, recollection of the sight should be amusing, yet it makes me shudder.

Confused, I fled and remained hovering at the top of the stairs, weeping while my father ranted at my mother below. She held him back from following me.

Something was my fault. I had caused this. I was in the wrong. I must be. Parents didn't do anything wrong—at least they never had before. I retreated to my bedroom and my Enid Blyton books. Hours later my mother came up and comforted me. My father had calmed down and the incident was never referred to. I resolved to be careful not to cross him in future.

On the 2nd December 1955 everything had changed. I was eight. I knew, in the way a child senses without being able to rationalise, that something had happened.

I knew there had been a car crash. The knock on the door. A policeman. 'I'm afraid there has been an accident.' A group of men who worked at the Atomic Weapons Research Establishment at Aldermaston had a car pool to and from work. An American driving on the wrong side of the road had hit the car in which my father had been a front seat passenger. The accident had not been a serious one and had just sent the car into a ditch. It was a new car and the driver had tried to get it out of the ditch by accelerating. The nearside wheels stayed in the ditch and the car cannoned into a telegraph post. Unrestrained by belt or bag, my father was flung through the windscreen.

His hat saved him from more serious injury. He stuck the part of his nose that had been sliced through back on and held it all the way to the hospital. It was stitched and he was sent home. Apart from this temporary re-arrangement of his facial features, he seemed to have been lucky.

In 1955, there were no brain scans. It was a full year before recurrent headaches led to his head being x-rayed and a fractured skull, broken cheekbone and damaged sinuses being diagnosed. He was in and out of hospital for several more years undergoing operations during which his eye was rolled out of its socket to gain access to internal organs. The possibility of brain damage was never mentioned.

He was awarded £1000 compensation four years later and replaced his pre-war Austin 8 with a gleaming black MG Magnette.

It was forty years after the accident before the full extent of his injuries was revealed. That year, after I had served lunch to both my parents, he had complained that he had not had anything to eat and had lunged at me with a screwdriver. My back was turned, I saw him reflected in a window and ducked. For years his anger had been brewing. He meant to hurt me. We arranged a private brain scan and an appointment to have the results analysed.

'Your father has frontal lobe damage of long standing', the psychogeriatrist told my mother and me almost as an aside. 'It almost certainly happened during the car accident.' The revelation was like a physical impact.

It finally dawned on me that my father had not been the only victim of that crash. I knew what had shaped my life since 1955.

As a child I was aware that there had been a change. I am not sure that I knew my father had changed or that the placid man who had left for work that morning would never return. No one told me he had suffered a personality transformation. I knew about the headaches because he told us he had them. I knew about the temper tantrums because they were directed at me. I just assumed it was my fault and that I could never please my father.

I sensed that if I were not there, my mother would be on the receiving end of his displeasure. He would turn on her in a way I had not seen, demanding aggressively that she answer for my 'attitude' towards him. I saw myself as her ally, but also as the reason why she was in trouble with him. I admired her for siding with me, not him. I felt a special closeness and warmth.

It was not constant, but the fear of incurring an impending rage was omnipresent. I became wary and cautious, confiding my observations to a diary.

'Daddy was really angry today. Took my boots and went out collecting planeria at the gravel pits with Chris. Played at 'Swallows and Amazons' all day. Came back.'

It was not that I thought he didn't love me. It was just that he loved me more than I thought I deserved. How could he love me when I didn't shape up?

That he did love me, I knew. And he told me he did. And I loved him. Unconditionally. That faltered, but fundamentally never changed.

Off I went to the cricket matches he was playing in. My mother would be a scorer. I would drift away to the edge of the field or the railway embankment to look at the trains. I wished I could be more interested. I should have been into sport. My father was a sports-man. But I wasn't. I scribbled some stories; some poems. I would rather have achieved ball skills on the field; wished I could; knew it was a failing in me, but I couldn't see the point. Still can't to this day.

Rages would spring from nowhere. 'Why won't he play cricket? I'd take him.' He arranged golf lessons.

'The boy's got a natural swing,' the pro told my father who proudly communicated this to his friends.

Yet hitting a small ball across grass held not much more appeal. The ideas that sprang from the pages of books were what I craved. I found refuge in reading and could get through a Doctor Dolittle and a Rider Haggard in a morning. Here was excitement and adventure that was for me more real than chasing a ball.

Perhaps, even at that early stage, I considered that

being simply competent would never have been acceptable. I did well at school. He was hugely supportive and there were few causes for complaint, but he would look around in other areas. His resentment simmered never far from the surface.

It is only by looking back, by analysing the minutiae of my father's life, that I can see how the damage simply escalated, although no one linked it with what had happened. The man who had been placid, jovial, spontaneous, became a driven workaholic.

The high standards he expected of himself were also directed towards me. Achievement had to be followed by a greater achievement. 'If you are doing a repetitive task, something you are used to, you can disguise the dementia that is building up', the psychogeriatrist would tell me years later.

There he was with undiagnosed damage and there we were dealing with dementia without ever having heard the word.

It was in that surreal instant of clarity, I knew that I had always been a carer; a protector; not only for my father, but for my mother as well. If you live with something long enough, it becomes the only reality. It never occurred to me to question it. Never considered the reasons why or even the effect it had on me. I had not known anything different.

It was only when this red-haired, black-robed, statuesque doctor looked over her pince-nez straight at me in her sun-filled room on that brilliant September afternoon in 1995 and said the words 'brain damage' that I made the connection.

'And it will get worse.'

She leaned back in her swivel chair, still looking directly at me. 'There will come a time when you will need to consider your options.'

Options? Were there any?

It was the first time I realised I may have already considered these. At the time when my contemporaries were moving out, I was building a house large enough to accommodate us all. My parents had had me late in life. My childhood had been full of friends, but I rarely if ever invited them home. I assumed there would be an awkward atmosphere, so avoided precipitating it. I went to see other people, visited them in their homes, did not take the chance of inviting them to mine.

A shame, in retrospect. My mother was a fine cook and would, under different circumstances, have loved to entertain.

That we did not was never an issue. It was a reality; simply a fact.

'No toys at the table, please.'

The collection was parked on shelves.

'Can I put my toy in my pocket, daddy?'

'Yes, Piers, but try and take it out before it goes through the washing machine again, won't you?'

'Are we having a boiling egg?'

'Yes, Lars, if you like.'

'I don't want one. I WANT one,' said Ian. 'Wazzat?'

'Your finger. Pointing.'

'No. It's milk.'

'You knew!'

Ian wriggled ecstatically on his chair and ran his sleeve under his nose. 'Dad, I don't want a banana.'

'That's OK, I haven't offered you one.'

'Yes, we have no bananas. We have no bananas today.'

'So what have we got, Piers?'

'We've got a nice juicy TOMARTO and a nice roasting POTARTO.'

'But?'

'We have no bananas today.'

'Can we have a little bit of television?'

'Yes, Lars, what would you like?'—'Bob Builder.'

Ian:—'I want 'Kipper'.'

Piers:—'Percy the Goal Keeper.'

'OK, we'll have one of each. We'll even have 'Percy the Park Keeper', shall we?'

'Then can we go outside for a little bit?'

'Yes. Lars.'

'It isn't snowing.'

'Quite right. There's a clear blue sky, so it's not likely to be snowing. But what's the weather like then?'

'It's not raining.'

'Can I have my wobbly ball?'

'Yes. Lars, you can have your rugby ball.'

Outside, the boys looked critically at their paired Wellington boots.

'Where's "puh" for Piers? Let me put them on daddy.' Each had memorised the first letter of his name from above his cot. Piers peeled the velcro from his slippers and squeezed each foot into the waiting Bob The Builder boot. He broke wind loudly as he contorted his small frame.

'Sorry, daddy. Farted.'

He noticed Pandora, the cat, lurking in the undergrowth, lilac fur conspicuous against the green, belly flattened, orange eyes on the lookout for something to kill. The previous day one of her victims had been presented to us in the kitchen, head dangling from a shelf; floor carpeted with feathers; wrenched off wing smeared across the table.

'Bird's sad,' Lars had observed. It was consigned to the incinerator. 'Is the bird hot now?'

Piers looked around for signs of the cat's ravages of the bird population.

'Nothing dead today,' he observed matter-of-factly.

3

The Nineties

Imperceptibly, my father had turned into a ticking bomb. His easygoing bonhomie no longer evident, worrying about his job took over.

Over the years, edginess slipped into paranoia; criticism into rages. Initially verbal, his aggression became physical, directed as much towards himself as to my mother and me. The raised hand and clenched fist were held up to my mother. Occasionally both made contact with me.

Harming himself became a familiar theme, sometimes accompanied by dire warnings about what he would do to us.

Push became shove which then became karate chop to the back of the neck in his later years if I let him get behind me in a temper. He would storm upstairs to his study, the words 'dead by morning' ringing in my ears—an empty threat, but devastating nevertheless. I remained awake until I heard him go to bed. I always locked my door, just in case.

He became obsessed with money that he claimed I

owed him, demanding written undertakings that it would be paid. He would create a scenario in which he had been defrauded. At length he wove the skeins into a conspiracy.

By the time we had analysed it all and removed the threats he perceived to his financial independence, he had forgotten the beginning of the chain of thought and the process started again.

On one occasion, he had polyps removed in hospital under general anaesthetic. When he came round, he was convivial; chatty. He told me about the other people in the ward. He was happy to introduce them, although he did not know their names. They were 'good chaps'. He beamed, delighted to have made friends.

He was alone in a single room.

Transferred to the local cottage hospital for convalescence, he was not the ideal patient. Convinced that he was being held against his will, he demanded to be released. 'It took two nurses and a hospital visitor to bring him down,' the ward sister told me over the telephone. He had made a bolt for freedom through a fire exit door while the staff had been occupied with a death a few beds along.

In the background I could hear his voice. 'You've got no right to keep me. I'll sue. Get my son.' Avoiding the edge of his hand to the back of my neck as I fastened his seat belt and telling him I was, in fact, his son and not the kidnapper he supposed me to be, I caught a glimpse of a face I recognised entering the hospital through the main door.

'They told me he had discharged himself and come home.'

One of his erstwhile golfing friends had come to visit him and had followed my car to the house.

'They seemed a bit "off" with me.'

I had just got my father settled in the sitting room. Convinced the friend had come to receive financial advice, my father took him through the basics of stocks and shares. The golfing friend never returned. There's nothing like mental illness to keep visitors away.

Always a competitive motorist, the possibilities posed by his powerful BMW sitting in the garage were not lost on us. He once disappeared for hours and returned minus a door mirror. His account of how someone else's dreadful driving had caused its loss changed each time he told it. He would sit behind the wheel pushing switches.

'There's something wrong', he would say. 'Only the headlights work.' We had hidden his car keys, claiming they were lost. When he located his spare, I loosened the battery connections and he assumed the battery was flat. Then we hid the garage door control unit. My father had become a problem of major proportions.

For years my mother and I had had no idea what to do. The police would regard such events as 'domestic' and not for their attention. Whatever happened in the home was a family matter, to be dealt with by the family. In this case, it was lived with. To disclose it would reveal a shameful inability to cope. It became accommodated into our lives. We managed as long as we could, pretending that we could accommodate his increasingly aberrant behaviour.

'We can't go on like this.' My mother was sitting on

the sofa regaining her breath. My father had stormed out of the house in a whirlwind of temper, knocking her flying. I picked her up and half carried her to the sitting room. I propped her up on her side with cushions.

'And it's not fair on you either, Ian. You should get more from life than him. You shouldn't have to put up with him.'

'But isn't there anything left? Now that you know why he's like this, don't you love him at all?'

She shook her head.

'No, there's nothing there. Not now. He shouldn't be here.'

'But he's not himself. He's ill.'

'And he's making us ill. He needs to be somewhere else.'

She it was who had told me what my father had been like before the accident. She it was who had found the old photos of us as a family. There I was being a toddler; being on a boat, being cuddled by my father, kicking a ball. Fragments of memory came back to me of his enormous love, times when he would throw me into the air in joy; when we would walk hand in hand; when he would read to me. That he had lashed out at me, I knew. I knew, too, that I had blotted out the memories so successfully that I could deny this even to myself. I can hardly bring them to mind even now. She had told me what a devoted father he had been. I knew that he had been intelligent, articulate and sensitive even after the accident during my formative years. This was the father I wanted to remember; wanted still to have.

Yet it was she who wanted him out. By every empirical standard, she was absolutely right, of course. But I loved him. She did not. That had died. She no longer recognised the man she had loved, the man she had married on the day before war was declared, and whose first meal alone with him was fish and chips on a blacked-out train, putting the bones out of the window. How she missed those days. By the 1990s the demons he had fought were taking him over.

I phoned around. Several homes baulked at the idea of taking him. Eventually I found one with a unit for the Elderly Mentally Infirm that was willing to take him on. I made arrangements, hating myself for doing this.

'It's just for a while so that you'll get better.' I was in the car driving him west to a place that seemed caring, understanding, able to cope. He looked straight ahead, sullen, resigned, tight-mouthed.

'Grrr.' He raised his left arm as though to cuff me. I ducked. The car twitched. It had just been a warning.

'It's for the best.' My mother had been watching Wimbledon on TV when I returned. She chatted brightly. A weight had been lifted. Always the pragmatic one, she had seen the problem and accepted that it had been removed. Not me. I remembered my father's words to me when I left.

'I know what you're doing. I won't forget this.'

My heart went out to him. I drove straight back to see how he was. He was where I had left him, in a room with a stable door. The top part was open. The bottom was locked. He had not stirred from his chair.

He had been given some food. Stains from it were round his mouth and down his lapels. He had wet himself. I talked to him, but he would not respond. He looked me hard in the eye. I was the one who had put him there and there was only hatred for me.

Some time later, I brought him home. Verbally aggressive though he remained, he did not touch my mother again.

Protecting her from him and protecting him from himself became my life. Unable to accept that it was the right thing to do, I had taken him out of the EMI unit. I took charge of both my parents. During the illness that preceded her death, I had to put my father back in a home. In six weeks he lost the ability to speak. Expensively provided for, he sat glumly in his single room. His only contact was with an elderly female resident who thought he was her husband and clutched his hand murmuring with cultivated vowels, 'Headley, Headley'.

I dreaded the visits, knowing that each time a little more personality had died. His body, too, was wasting into emaciation. I discovered that small amounts of food had been put in front of him and removed when he did not eat. A change of Home slowed the decline, but even so this was another waiting room for death. I would not have wished it for myself.

I popped in to visit him there early one evening to find him lying on his bedroom carpet in a pool of urine mixed with blood from a cut on his hand. He was making small movements, trying to get up. I looked down the corridor for help. No one there.

I lifted him up, changed him out of his soaked pyjamas, sponged him down, dressed him, combed his hair, put his teeth in and sat him in a chair. The staff told me he had been put to bed at six o'clock as they were short-staffed. So that he would not fall out, he had been moved to the floor. As I knew he always fell out of the same side of the bed at home, I had it shifted so that side was against the wall. It was something I had told the staff when he came in, but nothing had been done.

I wondered how long he would have laid there if I had not happened to visit him. Whatever restrictions this might place on my mobility, I knew that putting him in a Home in future would have to be an absolutely last resort. And I knew that I would have to visit frequently if I did.

To understand all is to forgive all.

Those few words from the psychogeriatrist had lifted the veil. He was a victim. What had happened to him was a tragedy. I knew that my love for him had been tested to breaking. I saw him as damaged, but indomitable.

My father was my responsibility. After my mother's death he was my only family. I wanted him near me. I wanted to look after him.

I brought him home. I thought I would need help. The employment of a resident carer—a frosty lady who confided to her friends in a letter she left inadvertently on my computer that she had 'reached the bottom of the heap'—was a terminated after a few weeks.

Two of the four others on the short list that resulted from my small ad in *The Lady* proved to have criminal convictions. A woman from an agency on a one week contract stayed half an hour—'He won't do as I say.' I knew then I would have to be the main carer.

A local agency sent sitters for an hour or two each evening. Only the really dedicated and talented returned. There was none better than Maggie. She would sing music hall songs from his era as she waltzed him round the hall. She held his hand, stroked his cheek and relished his wry smile. Of the three or four regulars, she was the one he loved. Putting him to bed after an evening with her was a dream, such was the calm she brought him. 'I'm a dying old man', he would repeat. 'Aren't we all, John?' she would respond. The truth was closer than we could have imagined. The day after she said this, in a terrible irony she died suddenly aged just 48.

Physically amazingly healthy and robust, I could see my father outlasting us all. Maggie had been supportive before the boys were born and loved them from the moment she saw them. I wish she could have seen them grow up. She was tearful when the story was broken to the newspapers. 'They've spoiled it. They always do, these rags. It was so lovely before they started in on you.'

When I read to the boys from 'The Velveteen Rabbit', their Christening present from her, about how love makes you real, I show them the post-it note she attached to the front page—'May you have much love in your lives'—and tell them this is a very special message from a remarkable lady.

The state is not sympathetic to the elderly mentally infirm. In West Berkshire at the end of the twentieth century there was no Day Care for someone like him. He was allowed to attend the Day Hospital locally on one day a week. This was seen as treatment not as care. When they decided they could do nothing for him, he was 'discharged'—cured.

Apart from me, there was no one to look after him, except at the weekends when St John's arranged a few hours respite, 'caring for carers' as they put it. It was removed when some of the ladies complained that he was too difficult for them. On weekdays, I employed a series of helpers.

They all fell away. My father could sense disengagement in an instant and reacted with stroppiness and the occasional punch, telling the unwanted visitor to leave. Whatever pains a carer may take to stimulate, entertain and show fellow feeling, there is little appreciation. For most, the job is one of containment only; there is not much satisfaction.

When the Human Rights Act was incorporated into English Law, I quantified my few hours a week of free time in a letter to the local Council. For whatever reason, day care was offered on three days a week. For the first time since long before the diagnosis I had the space to think about where my life was likely to go.

I was on my own. What to do? Something or nothing?

Knowing why I was in this situation was the trigger. I wanted to try to find out who I had been and who I would have been had circumstances been different. I felt I needed to go back to go forward; to feel what I had been like in 1955 before it all changed; to be a child again. I had to take myself to pieces and see what I really wanted. The closest I came—and it was an odd experience—was to find copies of some of the books I had read when I was eight. I managed to track down some examples of storybooks for children published in the early '50s.

They had the same dustjackets, the same pictures and even smelled the same as the books I recalled from that time. I became lost in the magic of Enid Blyton's 'Faraway Tree'. Silky, Moonface and Saucepan Man became real again. I was submerged in the memories and atmosphere that had helped shape me almost half a century before. I recalled myself as a happy only child with a vivid imagination.

I progressed to the Hardy novels of my teenage years and became lost in them again, their powerful passions mirroring the loves of my own life; their characters puppets on strings pulled by destiny.

I saw the same person with life somehow 'on hold', not free. The relationship that should have happened had not happened. I wished it had.

The answer came before finding a reason. It was clear—or at least let me know what I wanted. I wanted to have my own family.

Children, business, life—all they were all interconnected—inextricably so. My work as a teacher had always been with children.

On a general level, I had fought for their rights. In a personal context, I became very aware of children's development and shared their joy and that of their parents when they achieved individual and academic success. I changed people's lives, that was certain. But these were other people's children. Not my own. That was what I wanted. I wanted to see my own child develop.

I looked at dating agencies. The chance of meeting someone would be a fine thing. Yet to develop a relationship would take years and I was still a carer. My father could not be left alone for a minute. I would have to find someone much younger than me who could have children, unless I accepted the idea of an existing family. I had been with other people's children all my life in one way or another. I wanted my own.

Besides, marriage for the sake of having a child was doomed. I knew what I had to do; saw what was to be done. I would have a family of my own. As there was no one else, it would be on my own. Time was not on my side. I had better get on with it.

'Wanna go to the playhouse,' Ian demanded.

'What's the little word, you've forgotten?'

'Pleeease!'

Lars had already climbed the ladder to the playhouse.

'No. No!' Piers was yelling. Lars stood on the platform at the top of the ladder ready to apply a gentle boot to the climber.

'Get back, Lars.'

Lars retreated along the walkway to the top of the small stable door, tugging the handle. It remained shut. Only Piers could open it.

'Now you need him, Lars, don't you?'

Aware of his importance, Piers walked slowly to the door impervious to his brother's impatience. Two firm kicks to the lower section and the top door sprang open.

'Come up here, daddy. It's lunchtime.'

Dried leaves, pine cones, twigs and one of last season's conkers appeared in Ian's cupped hands.

'It's pasta. With tuna.'

A piece of branch appeared. 'And this is pudding. Banana.'

'Are we going to have nicies for dinner, daddy?'

'No, darling, the cats have nicies.'

The small table and chairs were dismantled and taken along another walkway to the castle.

'We're having a picnic.'

A gentle drizzle was falling.

4

Llanabba Castle

Recollecting in tranquillity, I went back through the stages to see where I had come from to reach this point and what had made me become so convinced that I could better rely on my own gut instincts than conventional wisdom. You are what you were. The past had shaped my thinking. Not until the newspaper articles much later did I think of my background as particularly unusual.

Not generally having the time, let alone the inclination, to indulge in introspection, I found the experience illuminating—although the outcome was prosaic. I saw myself as a succession of functions. Son, worker, carer... It seemed quite natural to add 'father'.

* * *

I had not intended to become involved with children's education. Far from it. The idea never entered my head. I had imagined a career in business with a multinational company. In those days, leaving university with an English degree was a passport to all sorts of jobs. I was spoiled for choice and decided to wait a while to see what I felt was right.

In the meantime, having enjoyed working on the Christmas post as an undergrad, I became a postman. Riding my GPO bike across the Berkshire countryside in the mellow late summer of 1968 gave me time to reflect. The various householders on whose doors I knocked with recorded deliveries chatted to me. Some of them wondered why this young man with a conspicuously RP voice was doing this job. 'Have you any…' (pause to find a word that wouldn't hurt my feelings) 'skills?'

'Qualifications, you mean? Oh yes, I can translate English into Anglo-Saxon.'

With skills so *recherché*, they were thrilled that I had found a job at the Post Office.

I decided to put my name down for supply teaching so that my academic background would not be completely wasted. It was all so simple. No checks. No references required. I phoned the local office and they rang me back. 'We've not had this sort of enquiry before, but a private school has rung up to see if we have someone on our books who can teach French. We see you did it at "A" Level.'

'As long as you can keep a few pages ahead of the boys, you'll do fine.' The Headmaster swirled his gown in a cloud of chalk dust and seated himself expansively.

Thus began what I anticipated would be a two week temporary teaching post at Crookham Court School near Thatcham. I would remain there for the next twenty years.

Llanabba Castle

* * *

When I started at Crookham Court in 1969, it was what Robert Smithwick had decided it should be when he started it up in 1961. Known locally as 'The Blind House' because of its boarded up windows, he gave life to the old building and started it as a small school for boys who were not great academic achievers and needed the security of an environment with small classes.

It was a public school in miniature. Chapel at the start of the day, then lessons, games every afternoon, more lessons, prep and the occasional outing. Traditional, solid, reliable.

The Houses were named after local rivers: Kennet, Avon, Enborne. I wondered why there were just three when four would have been easier for team games. The truth was that such a small school—Robert had thought in terms of 100 or so boarders—did not need a house system. The building was nuclear and the dormitories were grouped by age. The concept of House arose only in terms of sport and the Housemasters who assumed some pastoral responsibility for their charges. By and large, though, everyone knew everyone else and the boys gravitated to whoever appeared most congenial. In a building that was essentially stripped of the comforts of home, to take tea with a teacher, sit in a soft chair and feel carpet under the feet was enough of a treat to ensure that master's popularity.

The teaching was along traditional lines. Some of

the staff were well-qualified academically, some not. Modern teaching methods hardly applied here. On the notice board in Robert's room ('The Maths Room') was the admonition 'The Seeds of Education are Bitter, but the Fruit is Sweet'.

Robert was always 'The Commander'. He called his staff by surname alone. This was meant kindly. One addressed tradespeople with the honorific prefix. First names were not relevant here. Boys were surnamed by staff and by each other. Close friends would no more dream of introducing a first name than admitting their affection.

There were joint Headmasters. The Commander, known to me only after two decades as 'Robert', had started with a colleague who had left under a cloud a few years after the school started. The precise nature of the cloud remained a subject for speculation. Some preferred the thought of financial irregularity to that of moral lapse. We were very naïve in those days about such shortcomings.

In 1966, the Headmaster had appointed a new Head, Robby. 'Rave' as he was known, gave the place a touch of the Old School. He had come from Addis Ababa via Basingstoke. His Cambridge degree, flowing gown and fruity vowels gave reassurance of quality. A bon viveur and raconteur, his personality suffused the school. Parents were feted, flattered and left with the impression that their sons were in the groves of academia, that the cultured erudition emanating from 'The Study' and Rave's house, 'The Lodge', would be absorbed through the pores. The boys were less convinced. 'All piss and no shit' was the considered opinion of one of the Sixth Formers.

Dinners at The Lodge were protracted, wide-ranging and vinous. Ann, mini-skirted, kinky-booted, Swedish and flame-haired into her seventies, was a super cook and, when the cupboard was not bare—as it often was—her hospitality was extended to those few members of staff currently in favour.

On a clear summer's evening, her instructions to her daughter, 'AnYela, show ze Yentlemen into ze Yarden', could be heard through the windows of the school down the drive. The dramas and tensions when Rave was beaten around the head with a frozen fish were similarly common knowledge.

Much of my education was had over dinner in The Lodge. My throwaway 'Why do you serve a plate on a plate? Is it a quaint old Scandinavian custom?' was seized on with contempt. 'QVaint old Scandinavian custom indeed! Zis is Vat comes from not having been to ze best school or Oxford or Cambridge or dining in ze best houses' was her way of hinting to me that one never leaves an empty place in front of a guest. My dropping in through her letterbox the next day an article from a magazine to the effect that a hostess's duty is to make her guest feel welcome and at home went unremarked.

Her invitations continued, though. 'You must write a critique of ze Ballet Rambert for ze school magazine.' 'But I didn't go on that trip.' 'Vell, at least you Vill be unpreYuYiced.' I could see Angela squirm with embarrassment.

Often unwelcome at home and belaboured by frozen food, Robby was an isolated figure. Staff were picked up and dropped. In and out of his confidence they went. Down the hill to the ford I went in his car.

'I shouldn't tell you this.' Pregnant pause. 'In fact, I won't.' We drove back. He left in the summer of 1971 and never told me.

It was Llanabba Castle and *Decline and Fall* come to life. I loved it.

The microcosm of reality that is the world of the small private school took hold. As one of the few non-residents, I could take a detached view. They were all there. The adulterous French teacher, the manic Maths master, the lustful, the alcoholic, the derelict, the frustrated. In due course, like Paul Pennyfeather I found my own Margot.

By and large, the boys were educated and such was the sway the Commander held that no one questioned whether modern methods might have been more appropriate. His military training made him appear curt and decisive, as upright as his stance. Only once did he announce he was to give the boys 'shore-leave' instead of an *exeat*. 'It's the first time. I knew I'd do it sooner or later.' There was a chink in the armour.

The boys knew where they stood. They were disciplined. Manners were important. The day was structured and parents left the school to get on with its job. There was little money, but plenty of goodwill. The Parents' Committee—the 'Crookham Court Society'—met a couple of times a term for fund-raising activities and to give the boys treats. Crookham Court was doing what it had been set up to do. Somewhat shabby and in constant disrepair, no one really minded. Career teachers came and quickly went.

* * *

To supplement my meagre teacher's salary, I worked in the summer holidays. Robby had arranged with agencies—one German and one Italian—to recruit children to come over for a language-learning experience. He rented the school from the Commander and employed staff to teach and organise activities.

It was a simple arrangement. There were lessons, games and bopping to a record player in the evenings. I was a teacher and, although the two nationalities formed discrete camps, loved the international adventure.

In the summer of 1971, Robby fell ill with appendicitis. As the ambulance carried him down the pot-holed drive, he said to me 'Take over.' There I was, incredibly young, with the sudden responsibility for 60 children and 10 staff, some of whom were twice my age. I owe Robby a huge debt of gratitude. Disaster did not strike. The Course ran smoothly and we had a great time. Off went the children afterwards. I thought it would be fun to run the Course at the School again the following summer, but to do it with more than just two nationalities. A couple of the other teachers who had been working on the Course and taught in Madrid decided they would like to recruit students there, so we formed a partnership. It was called 'Educational Holidays'. I ran it from the spare bedroom of my home with a portable typewriter and a Roneo duplicator.

In fact, few of the students for the 1972 Course came from Madrid. Most of them were from the previous year or from friends of theirs who had heard about what fun it was and some were via Gabbitas-Thring, an educational trust that put parents who enquired about English Courses my way.

That summer, the Course was bigger and better. There were 72 students from lots of countries. The following year was even larger. I realised by this time that I did not need my partners. They recruited very few students, did none of the administration and did not keep much of a distance from the staff. The day the 1973 Course finished, I paid a visit to the Commander and arranged to rent the School myself in the summer of 1974. As soon as that had been achieved, I wrote to my partners dissolving the partnership.

The brochures were printed in November; two colours folded to fit a DL envelope. I was not allowed to do anything with them until my former partners had agreed a settlement, but in the middle of January 1974 I found myself free. It was like getting a divorce. On the day of my liberation, I posted the brochures. It was late, but not disastrously so. The Course was full within a few months. I loved being my own boss.

In 1974, I had more potential clients than places. People rang me almost apologetically some months before the summer on the off-chance that there might be a place left.

It was from the Netherlands that many of the students came. In the days when the disco was a gramophone and a few singles, the students tended to make their own entertainment. In this, we found the Dutch were remarkably inventive. They made things happen—one way or another. They were always exciting and sometimes outrageous.

A midnight pillow flight led to a boy being rendered unconscious. A call to his mother resulted in an interesting reaction. I had said I would expel him if he pillow fought again. His mother was a judge. 'I am not speaking "ex-cathedra"', she said, 'but I don't think you can do that. If he were fighting with a knife, then, yes, you could consider that his behaviour would render you incapable of performing the contract we have with you, but not with a pillow.'

We had to make the boy understand that there would be a dramatic consequence if he again tested our limits. Contractually, we could not take the action we wished. For want of any better solution, I removed everyone's pillow.

The result was a pillow strike. There was a minstrels' gallery around the dorms at Crookham. The students sat down in front of their dorms and refused to go to bed until they had their pillows back.

It was one of the first tests of my authority. I sent the staff to bed and took control. I closed the dorm doors on those few who were sleeping inside and stayed up until the early hours. Adrenalin kept me going longer than most of the youngsters. At 2 o'clock I told those who wished that they could go back to bed. By 3 o'clock, all of them had taken up my offer. The pillows were surrendered a few days later.

* * *

I was young—and looked even younger. I knew what I was doing—eventually—but it was not easy to get parents to take me seriously. There were inevitably moments when it counted against me for no obvious reason.

From my literature and letters, they had all taken me for older. Some could not conceal their disappointment when they met me. We had a Dutch boy whose parents stayed locally for a while until he settled in. After a week, they visited him.

'How's he doing.'

'Fine.'

'Any problems?'

'Not now that he's less competitive than he was. It was a problem when he used to get angry if he didn't win something, but now he doesn't bother and just joins in the games for the fun.'

'But he's good at most sports. What about his headaches?'

I was beginning to get the picture. Here was this boy with pushy parents desperately trying to please them. 'No headaches,' was my response. 'He reacts well to not having pressure on him.'

They departed, puzzled, but accepted that their son was happy and making friends. A few days later he was caught shoplifting. His parents returned, decidedly displeased.

'So what about your deep psychology now?' I didn't have a leg to stand on.

'Why was no one with him in the shop, supervising his purchases?'

'Making sure he didn't steal anything? Surely you don't do that at home.'

His mother had to agree. I could see no correlation between the removal of the desire to win and the dishonesty. His father, stung by the shame he felt his son had brought on him, saw it differently. Here was this trendy young educator telling the boy it was OK to lose. It was a short step to saying it was OK to lower one's standards; that low standards were acceptable; that having low moral standards was perfectly all right. The successful and ambitious son he had brought had been turned into something quite the opposite by me.

'You have made my son a criminal,' were his final words.

Into my life came more and more children. To look after them, organise them, give them a great time and prepare them for the future was becoming second nature to me. But I still loved teaching and stayed on at Crookham Court.

* * *

Whatever Robby may have given by way of airs and social graces, his successor as Headmaster, David, did not choose to display. A Quaker and a northerner, he looked at the little world he had come to control out of deep-set eyes and rejected its pretensions.

The Commander was at the stage when he wanted to hand over control of the day-to-day affairs and assume a bursorial role. David was the sort of down-to-earth fellow he felt he could leave to get on with it. Married and with two young children, David looked at modern methods, suggested that staff should go on Courses, introduced a measure of pupil power and, while leaving the ethos of the school undisturbed, set about giving it more relevance to the type of pupil it was seeking to attract. As Crookham Court edged forward and numbers kept up, Robert and David achieved a mutual respect while the School gradually lost its Waughian quality.

Cancer came suddenly to David. He felt a slight ache under his arm while driving the boys to an archery match in the minibus one Sunday afternoon. He found the lump that he thought was the cause and went to the doctor without delay. Test followed test. His decline was swift. From being a sporty, six-footer in his mid-thirties, within a year he was on his back in hospital. His mind keen, alert, articulate. His body deteriorating, useless, skeletal. The irony was not lost on him. He was not a man to harbour grudges, but he resented his inexorable decay. 'It's all right here.' He pointed to his head. 'It's just that I can't do anything with this.' He lifted his arm to indicate the body that lay on the bed.

This was the first and only time that he came close to mentioning the inevitability of his death or of giving in to despair. With a typical stiff-upper lip, everything thenceforth remained unsaid. It was unmentionable. Illness had never before intruded into David's life. He never smoked, hardly ever drank, was not one to feel stress, was active, happy and positive about what he was doing. Now his body was crumbling and he could see it.

Even more cruel was the remission. For just a few weeks, he returned home and came into to the School. We were seduced by hope. Within the month he was dead.

For Robert, the Commander, this was the start of real problems. He had come to depend on David. The job of running the school, the job that Robert had no interest in, was now his burden. It was just work. The financial reward was negligible.

Robert's wife, Rosemary, had died in December 1969. The date remains clear in my mind. It was the night of the Christmas Dinner. Someone joked that from the 13 of us sitting down to dinner on the 13th, one would not make it through the night. She was taken to hospital with double pneumonia just after the meal and died in the early hours. The grip Robert had on his emotions was as tight as his clenched fist that morning.

'Let the parents know the Carol Service has been cancelled and that they can come and collect the boys when they wish'.

'Is there anything else we can do?'

'That's kind, but no'.

'Can we take the boys out somewhere?'

'No, I like to have them here.'

Angela and I interpreted loneliness as self-sufficiency. Robert had never made an art out of expressing feelings. We had come to think of him as not possessing them.

Shortly after David's death, his wife phoned me. It was after midnight and she needed to talk.

'He proposed to me.'

'Who?'

'Robert.'

'What did you say?'

'I said "no". It's just too soon. He said that he couldn't run the school on his own.' It was that brief.

For a moment a possible future for Crookham Court School had flickered. His timing was hopeless. The flame was snuffed out and in that moment another future for Crookham Court had started to crawl from the ashes.

1977 was the year of the Silver Jubilee. It was a time for celebration, but for Crookham Court it was the point at which everything changed. The Crookham Court Society sensed that Robert was disenchanted with Crookham. He had said more than once that if someone made him an offer, he would sell. We had not believed it then, but we believed it now. The idea of a purchase was raised. Several of the parents could have afforded it, but before a plan could be drawn up, Robert announced that he had sold the School.

He was guarded about his successor. 'I've made way for an older man', he said. 'He plans to take a back seat in the running of the School and will have a different style from mine'.

Robert was always terse, but the staff were curious. After all, they and the boys had been sold along with the School and everything in it.

'He has been invited to Speech Day, but is rather shy and has declined'.

We wanted to meet him, to get the measure of

him—this man who was to take us over. All we found out before the start of the Autumn Term in 1977 was his name.

It was a sign of things to come and Llannaba Castle was no more.

'What we having? Is it pasta?'

'Yes darling. Now, no toys at the table. Toys on the shelf.'

Three small bodies heave themselves into their chairs.

'Wazzat, daddy?'

'Cat pooh.'

'No it's not. It's pasta.'

'You knew! You're just testing daddy.'

Ian lowered his head and raised his large blue eyes. A smile crept from side to side.

'And the sauce? ...'

'It's cat wee wee.'

'Yes, Piers. How did you guess?'

My three small sons wielding their Fimbles spoons and forks into their Fimbles bowls, scoop up the coated fusili. A picture of normal twenty first century childhood. Almost.

Like an Anglo-Saxon riddle, these are boys who have no mother, yet they have two. Their father and mother met, but after they were born. The mother who bore them is no relation. They have five siblings of whom one is no more and four are unborn.

5

Mother

My mother had been a *couturière*. She could sketch a design in seconds. Her deft fingers at the sewing machine transformed mere fabric into stunning creations. She loved the buzz of London life and her frequent flights to Paris. Talented and beautiful, she slipped into her glamorous life with relish. My earliest recollections are of a slim, elegant figure. 'My mother's a lady. You're a woman', I blithely told one of the several nannies who came and ere long went.

'I think your son needs you,' the doctor had told her when I was three. 'Your constant presence may help him overcome his stammer.'

Without giving it a further thought, she stopped work. The nannies disappeared. So did her income. She expressed no regret. My father had gained promotion in the civil service and they moved out of London to Newbury in Berkshire where he worked at the Atomic Weapons Research Establishment in Aldermaston and she cultivated a small clientele at the US Air Force base at Greenham Common who appreciated bespoke women's fashion.

Stunningly de mode in comparison with my friends' mothers, her love and care shaped my life. She was an artist who translated her ideas into sketches and her sketches into creations. I loved the colours and feel of the fabrics that came into the house—a contrast to the grey austerity and rationing that was post-war Britain.

As the days of domestic staff had gone, my mother kept the house going and saw to me during the years my father was in and out of hospital for the operations that sought to cure his headaches, delighting in my successes and commiserating over any setbacks.

Although practical to a fault, she could be delightfully dizzy. Back in the days when you simply parked in town at the side of road and did not think to lock your car while you were shopping, my father and I found her sitting in the back seat of one parked several cars away from our own. He tapped on the window and she wound it down. 'Whatever are you thinking of? This isn't our car.' 'Well, it was black like ours,' she said later by way of explanation. 'But the seats were green! Ours are red.'

Years later I would drive her to the Post Office on market day each week to collect her pension. Yellow lines now flanked the roads. Car parks were on the town's periphery, not within walking distance for her. I would drop her, drive round and collect her. One day, I was at the traffic lights just along from the Post Office. I saw her waiting for me on the pavement. A small black hatchback stopped in front of her, caught in the traffic. My mother disappeared through the passenger's door. She reappeared a few seconds later, mouthing apologies to the driver. 'Well, it was the same colour as yours.' 'But mine's big with four doors!'

She took her driving test six times. On the day she passed, my father let her take the wheel. She leapfrogged ten yards and stalled.

'Ian drives,' he said, opening the door for her. She never drove again.

* * *

We never discussed it in great detail, but we knew what we were up against with my father. Whenever anyone remotely marriageable came into my life, her unspoken fear was evident. It was in her eyes; in every movement. Without the need for her to say a word, she was terrified that I would leave her alone with the man she had fallen out of love with and now saw as an implacably hostile force in her life.

The thought of leaving my father was dismissed out-of-hand. She had made vows for better or worse. For those of her generation, it was her duty to stay. So I did. Together we dealt with my father, ran the house, the business, the cats. We became a team. When diverticulitis set in, I took over some of the more physical work she had done. She was a great survivor. On the day of her discharge from hospital after a minor operation, a routine blood pressure test revealed that she had no blood pressure. She had had an aortic aneurism. That she was already in hospital was what saved her life. We went through the roller-coaster of emotions that the life-and-death environment of the Intensive Care Unit engenders. My father had to come with me. He was shocked by the knowledge that something had changed; uncomprehending quite what it was. Her recovery was complete, but we knew what a fine line there was between being alive and being dead.

* * *

Five years later, we found how fine that line was. She had felt unwell for several months. during my busy summer period. We decided we would have to put my father into a Home for a few weeks while she went into hospital to see what was wrong. A straightforward operation was recommended. She walked into the Royal Berkshire Hospital in Reading wearing a beige trouser suit of her own creation. I requested private treatment, but was told that the operation would be performed on the NHS by the same surgeon who would have performed it privately and was reassured. The surgeon I had been promised did not perform the operation. It went horribly wrong and she spent over a week in intensive care, unconscious, hovering between life and death.

I was there every day. On 27 September 1999, I was told to prepare for the worst. She was unresponsive. They suspected brain damage. I asked them if they had checked her hearing aid. The nurse I spoke to had no idea she wore one. I turned it on, cleaned it, adjusted it, took her hand in mine and spoke directly into her ear.

'Don't die,' I pleaded. 'They're starting to give up on you. Come round. Show them you understand. Squeeze my hand.'

She squeezed. A nurse came over.

'She squeezed my hand. She can understand!'

'Will you please stop talking so loudly about dying. You'll upset the patients.'

'But they're all unconscious.'

'And you'll have to leave as this is the period when the patients have deep rest without visitors.'

I paced the corridors. When I returned, her eyes were open. She was sitting up. He mouth moved. She was saying my name. We sat together for hours. I drove home elated and hopeful.

Just after midnight, I was telephoned to say that a 30 year-old woman needed to be admitted and that, if someone needed to be admitted to intensive care, the fittest patient had to leave. My mother was 87. That they considered her suddenly 'fit' came as a welcome surprise. I believed them. That the hospital mentioned the age of the incoming patient should have sounded a warning note. My mother was duly moved out of intensive care back to the ward and was dead within the day.

How I regretted bringing her into consciousness that day. That was all that had marked her out as fit. We had been left alone for most of the day. I was holding her hand. Her breathing became shallow and faded to nothing. I kissed her on the forehead, left the bedside and told the nearest nurse that my mother had died. Never have I felt so powerless.

'Go on. Go to pieces', a visitor had urged me, noticing my composure. But there was no longer anyone to pick them up again.

* * *

There is a kind of serendipity in adversity. On the last day my mother would ever spend at home, an old friend whom I had not seen for some years, another Ian, visited me. He had phoned to tell me his me marriage was collapsing and wanted to talk it through. I was not sure what I could contribute but was happy to be a listener.

His arrival had been fixed some days in advance, but it coincided with my call to the doctor asking that my mother be taken to hospital. It was a crisis for me. Ian was having his own crisis. Over the next few weeks, we spoke frequently. In different ways, our lives were collapsing. I valued his support and we spoke frankly about feelings. He was desperately trying to rescue his marriage. I was feeling the lack of having one.

It was on the day of my mother's funeral that Ian propelled me in the direction of the internet. He had stayed for the weekend and was getting me to search out dating agencies. I filled in some forms. I knew that I would shortly be taking my father out of the nursing home and having him back with me. The pain of separation was becoming unbearable.

How could I meet these women? I knew it would make life tough for me, but I felt a huge responsibility towards my father. Where would I find the freedom to develop relationships? Who would want to share my life as a carer for a charge who was difficult, demanding, and unrewarding to everyone but me?

'I wonder', I mused aloud, 'if there are any surrogate mothers on the web.'

'One way to find out,' said Ian.

I tapped the magic word into Lycos. There they were smiling out at me from cyberspace. None was in this country. Most had addresses in Texas or further west. I wondered how they went about surrogating. What was surrogacy about? How did you get started?

The only agency the search engine I was using came up with was in Los Angeles. The site was attractively presented and clearly written. Its title was a clever one—'Growing Generations'. Even I could understand that it was done by artificial insemination, either with the surrogate's own egg or with one bought from an egg donor. I gathered it was run by gay people, but it seemed to exist for all single people as well as gay singles and couples.

'Make a date for an appointment,' Ian suggested. He had seen the smidgen of optimism through the sorrow. 'We'll have a trip to California. You've got nothing to lose.' I e-mailed for literature and phoned for an appointment. It all seemed so easy. I felt I was getting somewhere without being quite sure where.

Growing Generations' Sandi Greenberg was coolly efficient over the phone. The date arranged was Friday 12 November 1999. I was to meet Gail Taylor and Will Halm, the chief executives.

Ian decided to come along. If nothing else resulted, we would have a pleasant enough long weekend break in California. I employed a carer to look after my father at home for a few days. On the Wednesday before, we flew to Los Angeles.

6

Growing Generations

I reached California full of trepidation about the enormity of what I was about to undertake. The clear blue skies and brilliant sunshine of Los Angeles airport on that day in early November 1999 did not make it any easier.

It was the awfulness of the Avis rental car that unsettled me first. There it sat with slanted headlights and deep ribbed panels along its flanks, lurid in metallic jade. The smell of vomit-mixed-with-apple-blossom that characterises American plastic exuded from its interior. East? West? Where was the sun setting? Grid-like and logical the American road system may be. Well-signed it is not. All the directions were to go east or west. OK if one knows which way east or west is. There were some hills in the distance, so I guessed the Beverley Hills Hilton lay among them. I headed for them through the evening rush hour traffic, past Hispanic areas and run-down ghettos. At least the Pontiac did not sound as though it was about to break down in one of these very grim and destitute-looking neighbourhoods.

By the time we reached the hotel, I had worked myself up into a panic. 'It's all horrendous,' I said. The huge, gothic limos, the garish buildings, the noise, the truncated staccato speech patterns, the busyness, the vulgarity of it got to me. 'I can't do it.'

Ian brought me back to reality. 'You haven't done anything yet'. He went out to explore the hotel. Rather than listen to the nasal inflections of the arguing couple in the next room, I busied myself calling reception and requesting a change of room. It was handled with the mechanical efficiency that I had become used to. By 8 o'clock, I was ready for bed. I woke at 2 and watched 'The Wonder Years' until dawn, waited for the breakfast room to open at 6.30 and prepared for the day ahead.

'We do not validate parking' said the instructions on the Growing Generations fax telling me where they were. It was a foreign language. I drove east—or was it west?—until I failed to find Wilshire Boulevard as the first intersection. Had no one noticed the missing 't', I thought as I three-point turned against the traffic?

Wilshire turned into La Cienega which turned into something else and back into Wilshire. Fortunately I had allowed two hours for the few minutes' drive and arrived at San Vicente with an hour to spare.

I found that 'we do not validate parking' did not mean that it did not exist. It was just that I had to pay for it. As everywhere in Los Angeles, underground car parks support each building. To kill time, we walked the immaculate pavements, the only pedestrians, expecting a soaking from the hidden sprinkler systems keeping each verdant lawn from succumbing to the constant heat.

At the appointed hour, we entered Growing Generations building. It was starkly modern and meant business. I realised that GG was a gay-run operation. Ian and I had wondered if we would be taken for a couple. We idly speculated that it might make life easier if we were taken as one. Neither of us is into that sort of deception, though, and while we did not state that we were not linked—the question did not arise—we did not announce our status on arrival. I thought that in California anything goes.

We were greeted by Teo Martinez, a tall, bronzed young man with a gentle handshake and ushered into a room dripping with photos of happy parents and babies. Single men, single women, single babies, two babies, two men, two women. We got the picture. The two founders of Growing Generations, Will Halm and Gail Taylor, entered.

They were charming, informative, announced their gay and lesbian status and talked through their programme. I had no idea why a woman would wish to become a surrogate and I am not sure that their explanation made me much wiser. That would come later. They described their surrogates as 'mavericks', leading lives that were unconventional with relationships that could be complicated, but all of whom, it seemed, loved babies.

What was necessary, it was stressed, was to build up a relationship with the surrogate. To meet and meet again, to discuss every aspect of the pregnancy before and during it. To come over to renew the relationship, to deliver fresh sperm, to maintain the interest, to support the woman at every stage. It sounded like hard work and the element of angst was never far away. My suggestion of frozen sperm was met with a reasoned comparison of the virtues of fresh versus frozen rather along the lines of carrots. Fresh was determined to be far better.

There was then the question of the egg. The surrogacy could be the insemination of a surrogate or it could be gestational with the surrogate being implanted with a fertilised egg that came from another woman, an egg donor. After the description of the average surrogate who I pictured leading a life of near-lawlessness on the wrong side of the tracks, I had quite decided I did not want to take a dive into that gene pool. A nice college graduate egg donor was infinitely preferable. It did not appear that I would also have to strike up a relationship with her.

Then it was my turn. I was asked how many children I wanted. 'Oh, the more the merrier', I ventured. I had thought the light-heartedness had been evident in my tone of voice. Not in California.

More angst on the perils of a multiple birth for the surrogate. OK, I would be thrilled with one. What sort of business did I run, what could I offer a child? They were building up a picture of me as someone they either would or would not welcome on their programme. All was going well.

'In eighteen months or two years, you'll be a parent,' said Will Halm. 'You'll make an excellent father.'

I thought the deal was done.

* * *

'But how do you think your clients will view all this?'

'They trust me with their children. It will have no effect.'

'But what about when you come out? We don't have people staying in the closet.'

'Coming out as what? What closet? I realised you were a gay organisation, but I didn't think you dealt only with gays. Won't you deal with someone who isn't gay?'

'Our surrogates only do it for gay people. That's what motivates them.'

'But you've said that I would make an excellent parent. If your surrogates trust your judgement, surely one will accept your word that I'm suitable.' I was desperate. I could see it all slipping away.

'We have two Englishmen whose surrogate is about to give birth to twins. We have secured the right that both men be named on the birth certificate as parents. That's a major achievement. You can see it on our video.'

What I had thought was an organisation that enabled children to be born was more complicated than this. It appeared to be almost a by-product of the real aim which was to present gay families as being as normal as heterosexual families. That was the drum they were beating and I was marching to a different tune.

The mood in the room changed. The silence was awkward. It was clear I was out on my ear.

'We could recommend you elsewhere.'

'But I'm here for just another couple of days and tomorrow's Saturday.'

I imagined that another agency would take me down the same tortuous track. I gave them my mobile number and we left. I really thought I had blown all my chances. It occurred to me that perhaps under Californian law they couldn't discriminate against non-gays, but I knew that I would not test this out.

* * *

Already arranged to follow my appointment with Growing Generations was a visit to Reproductive Technology Laboratories ten miles away in Santa Monica to leave a semen sample. The Pontiac smelled even more of vomit. I was on autopilot. As we drove along the Boulevard with the 't' missing, I said to Ian, 'What's the point? If there's no surrogate, there's no reason to go to this place.'

We were supposed to head west to Sepulaveda. When that failed to appear, we realised we had been heading east. I phoned to apologise for being late. The US service culture switched into action. No problem. 'What the hell. There's nothing else to do'. We drove on and swept into the underground garage beneath RTL's building. Both of us went to their office. We were invited to go into their special room. 'Oh, Ian wants to do some shopping, thanks. It's just me.' In I went.

As we had come from Growing Generations, the room had been specially prepared. On the TV was a fuzzy videotaped image of two well-endowed young men wearing nothing but chains vigorously trying to remove them from each other. I looked away and studied the dark blue sofa and carpet. They were perfectly clean. No tell-tale stains. I dropped my clothes onto them and stood in this perfectly normal reception room in an utterly bizarre situation thousands of miles from home and a world away from everything I was used to. 'Abstinence for at least three days' had been the instructions from RTL. It took me no time to deliver the goods and I left the two young men, now unchained, to explore their chafe marks. I presented my pot to the charming lady at the counter and watched her label it. Would I ever see the contents again?

'Well that's a waste of time', I said to Ian. I hummed 'I left my heart in San Francisco' and changed the words to 'sperm in Santa Monica'. We drove along the sea front and then back to Beverley Hills. It was 8 pm. Time for bed. I threw up all night. It had all been too much.

To kill time while hoping my mobile would ring with some alternative agency, we spent the next day at Universal Studios in Hollywood. Ian was more optimistic than I was. My phone had remained silent. 'One day we'll come back here with my daughter and your child'. I did not believe it.

Back home in Britain, I e-mailed Will Halm asking him to re-consider. No chance. He told me he had mentioned me to a woman called Vivian Leslie and that I would hear from her. I waited for a week, then I did.

7

Vivian

I liked Vivian from the start. It was not just that she might offer me what I wanted. It was her whole approach to the concept that was such a change. Gone was the angst.

'What about a surrogate?'

'I'll fax you a profile.'

'What about a donor?'

'I'll e-mail you some pictures and fax you their profiles, too.'

'But don't I have to come and give fresh supplies?'

'Fresh, frozen, it's all the same. But it would be good for you and the surrogate to meet. Why don't you invite us?'

Oh, yes, I liked Vivian more and more. Her agency was Surrogate Family Program, now Fertile Ground as she could not register her former trading name. The faxes came grinding in. The surrogate was the easy part. One had stood out in Vivian's mind. Tina's profile came in on 7 January 2000.

Q: Would you be a traditional surrogate using the artificial insemination procedure?

A: No.

Q: Would you be a gestational surrogate using the IVF procedure?

A: Yes.

Q: Would you be a surrogate for a gay couple?

A: No.

Q: Would you be a surrogate for a single dad?

A: Yes.

Q: If I could change one thing in my life it would be:

A: That my children knew my mom, their grandma. And for my mom to be able to see the beautiful babies that I brought into the world.

Q: The person that I admire most is:

A: 'My mom. She taught me so much and gave me so much love and strength to grow on. I will never admire anyone more than I admire her.'

Q: What goals have you set for yourself?

A: 'I have so many goals that I hope to accomplish for my children and myself. My most recent goal is to provide a loving environment for my children to grow up in. I guess this has been my main goal since my children were born.

Q: How are you teaching your children the value of money?

A: Because of the fact that I am a single parent of two boys, unfortunately my kids are very aware of money value. They understand that you must earn money. It definitely doesn't just come to you. So by my being honest with them about bills and income, they are learning to value the money we have.

Great. The clincher was 'I have always wanted to…' and she answered '… travel around to different places like the Hawaiian Islands or go on an airplane. That probably sounds funny, but I have never been on one.'

I determined that Tina was about to visit Isles rather to the north of Hawaii, and that she would, indeed, get to go on a plane. We had some preparation to do first, though.

Vivian needed the answers to various questions as to why I wanted to be a parent, a brief financial statement and a photo. I needed to find a donor. Almost as an afterthought, I felt I should also discover what the English legal situation was with regard to surrogate babies.

Finding a donor was easy. Vivian e-mailed me a selection of delights. Most were brown-eyed and dark. One, 'ED (Egg Donor) #211,' was gorgeous. She stood out as a real English rose. Vivian described her as 'Very beautiful, has modelled, has very petite figure. Men can't take their eyes off her and women want to be her. Very modest, doesn't seem to know just how lovely she is. Very brainy too, has Masters degree in Civil Engineering.'

She was certainly the one. She was in demand and I had to wait my turn. Her detailed profile was faxed to me and showed that she was from a healthy family as well as being bright. I knew all about her, even to the medical history of her grandparents, but had no idea of her name. I decided to call her 'Edie' after her number.

Vivian

* * *

Finding out about the English legal situation was more complicated. It was just as well that I waited or I might never have started.

My own solicitor could not begin to help me. What I was asking about was not precedented in English Law. He suggested a firm of specialists in family law in the west country, but they could not help. The case of the 'gay dads' had just made the headlines in the UK. I noticed a caption in one of the papers which read 'One egg, two babies—but how many parents?' Curious to know the answer, I made contact with the writer, a solicitor. We met. The 'fun' began.

While he could not advise me on any contractual arrangements in America, he was able to tell me what I needed to do to make sure that I was legally the father. English law in 2000 predated DNA testing, so the mother is the person who gives birth—even if she is not the biological mother. The father is the mother's husband if she is married, even if he is not the biological father.

It defies the logic that DNA testing would provide, but it was within this imperfect framework that I had to arrange my life. Had I been a woman, the babies would have right of residence and would be British. Because I am a man, they would have neither of these advantages. Tina was married. Her husband had decamped two years before she and I made contact, abandoning her and her two sons, Matthew and Ryan. Before anything happened, she would need to be unmarried, so Tina had to get a divorce.

This was no sacrifice for Tina. Her husband had become a 'dead-end dad', as she called him. The problem was how to contact this vanished man. The instant divorce that I had assumed was the norm in the US turned out to be a myth in our case. It took some time for the various papers to be signed and for the legal wheels to turn. Absolutely nothing could happen until that moment. At least it gave Vivian, Tina and me the time to meet.

In her e-mail to me, Vivian looked forward to getting 'aquatinted'. I thought it was an American pun. She told me later it was just bad spelling.

Tina had expressed her desire to fly, so I bought tickets for her to come over with Vivian. It was odd meeting them at Gatwick. There is no established etiquette for greeting the future mother of one's surrogate children, but fortunately we established a good understanding from the start.

Tina had one major concern. 'As a nurse, I see death on a daily basis. What happens if you die?' she asked. She was eminently sensible and realistic. I knew this was no maverick. I was dealing with an intelligent woman whose head was firmly attached to her shoulders. I explained the role of the Foundation I had created and that I planned that one of its functions would be to oversee my offspring in the event of my early death.

I had many questions for her. The main one, of course, was to find out why she wanted to be a surrogate. I was still concerned about the headstrong, unconventional, sailing-close-to-the-wind impression

I had been left with by Growing Generations. Tina was frank and direct. She had followed her instinct in wishing to work in a hospital, but she had seen marriage as a way to leave home, married early and unwisely and her life had been sidetracked. Here was a chance to become someone special, to do something out of the ordinary and thus to rise above the norm. She also liked being pregnant.

Good. Everything seemed so straightforward with her.

'But would you do this with your own egg?'

'No, I couldn't give away my own child.'

'How about having more than one child? What would you think about this'.

Here we were on less certain ground. In principle, Tina had no problem with having twins.

Vivian described how the egg donor would be stimulated with drugs to produce many eggs. These would be fertilised and a number would be implanted into the surrogate. If more than the desired number took, the excess could be reduced.

'Reduction'. An innocent term. The baby, Vivian told us would 'have a demise'—a gentle concept that hid a stark reality. 'Basically', she said, raising a fork to her lips at lunch in a fashionable Marlborough restaurant, 'the one nearest the needle gets it through the heart.'

Having a demise was clearly more drastic than having a slight chill. Abortion is killing no matter how euphemistically it is dressed up.

Neither Tina nor I were comfortable with the idea of killing babies. We thought twins would be nice, but we would be happy with what we got. Abortion was ruled out. Vivian and Tina introduced me to The Fairy Shop in Marlborough in case I had a daughter. I took them to the Royal Shakespeare Theatre in Stratford-upon-Avon. Vivian was striking in her pink jump suit. I provided a contrast in my sober jacket. We were all three quite different in our backgrounds, but about babies we saw eye-to-eye. There was no doubt that we wanted to go ahead.

'Have I passed the test?'

'Oh, yes. It isn't like that at all'.

But I am sure it was.

8

Watership Down

The solicitor was keen to acquaint me with those aspects of English law that covered surrogacy. I met a QC in Chambers to find out more. The laws on surrogacy had not been tested in English courts. It is not that it is illegal; it is just that agreements on the subject are contractually unenforceable. The surrogate mother would have every right to keep the baby. British law on egg donation is that such provisions cannot be bought. It would be a question of making private arrangements for a woman to be artificially inseminated and for her to produce my baby with her own egg—no one else's. If she were already married, I would not be the father. The choice of characteristics that would determine half of the baby would be limited.

The only option was to take advantage of the freer climate in California. Nevertheless, I would receive no help from the courts in this country so far as the Californian contract was concerned; whatever papers were signed in California, would have no meaning here. Tina would sign away her parental rights, but such a waiver would be irrelevant here.

In theory, Tina could claim the baby as hers. It would not matter that she was not the biological mother. She could even claim child support from me All she had to do was arrive in the UK. Tina had to know her legal rights in this country and I told her them. She assured me that there would be no problem. She already had all the family she wanted. It would be my baby.

Rather than bring the baby in from America with a US passport and have to go through the process of applying for residence, I needed to find out if Tina would be willing to deliver the baby over here. I told her I would arrange for her sons to go to school. I took her to see a prestigious local prep school. She fell in love with the house, its sunken formal gardens and its grounds sweeping along to Watership Down. She thought it would be a great opportunity for her boys. I was sure of it, too, having set up several international educational programmes. Everything was going swimmingly.

It was clear that Tina would be an ideal surrogate. Almost as an afterthought, Vivian suggested, just in case the birth happened to be in the US, that I should take out a US-health insurance policy with an American company that also enabled one to cover one's dependents at birth. I took her advice and arranged cover before anything was started. It was very cheap. A single Englishman living in England was statistically unlikely to acquire unhealthy American dependants.

The IVF clinic Vivian worked with was The Smotrich Center for Reproductive Enhancement in La Jolla, California. Before anything could happen, I had to have a blood test to ensure that I was not harbouring any nasty diseases.

The trouble was that, to have a blood test, I had to have a referral from my doctor. To get a referral, I would have to disclose why I wanted a blood test. I was not sure that a doctor could refer me for a blood test in order to proceed to what may, for all I knew, have been an illegal act. I certainly did not want to make anyone in this country aware that I was embarking on a surrogate pregnancy programme. It was a dilemma.

How about becoming a blood donor, Vivian suggested? They would surely test my blood first and I could use this to show Dr Smotrich I was clear. A few enquiries revealed that there was a blood donation session in Hungerford the following day. Imbued with a feeling that although my aims were selfish, I was also doing also something good, I drove there, filled in the forms and waited hours to deliver my armful.

'We can let you have a certificate saying you are a blood donor' was the response to my request for some sort of statement as to what the blood had been screened for. That was not what I had in mind. In fact, when I ran through the list of diseases, I found that several were not in the test.

I then asked a hospital in Windsor if they would accept a referral from a doctor in the US for a blood test for insurance cover. No problem. All he had to do was to fax his request. I asked Dr Smotrich to do this and he faxed me back a copy. 'Please draw the following tests for Ian Mucklejohn' it read. A list of various hepatitis and HIV-related tests followed. The last line read 'semen analysis with morphology'. What a giveaway! I contacted the Smotrich Centre. They agreed that they would analyse my frozen sample and would re-fax the hospital with a list that excluded the semen analysis in the hope it would be seen as an error. Back came the revised fax. It was identical to the previous one except that the words 'semen analysis with morphology' had been scratched out and the words 'please disregard semen analysis' were inserted.

I expected a phone call from the hospital at any moment to enquire about the exact purpose of the tests. But instead, the only one who contacted me was Smotrich who wrote 'I received the blood work today. I will be meeting with Tina on June 12th to start her on the first set of medications and with your donor on June 19th to start her on Meds. I anticipate the actual procedure to be the first week in July. Take care.'

I was clear to proceed at last.

9

Crunch Time

While I could see ahead to the horizon, the road was cratered with potholes. Tina was still not a free woman. If we continued with the procedure while she was still married, the child would not be mine. Her husband had disappeared and she had to track him down through his relatives.

He was in another state when Tina filed her petition, which was fine. But he was also in jail. My mind raced. My only contact with America's 'correctional institutions', as they euphemistically call them, was through a prisoner called Jeff to whom I had been writing for the past ten years via a UK organisation called 'Lifelines'. It exists to put people who have nothing to look forward to in their lives in touch with those who will maintain a correspondence with them. He was on Death Row awaiting the ultimate correction—execution. Through Jeff's letters, I had acquired an awareness of the inhuman conditions in these places and the sort of people whey contained. What sort of criminal was Mr P? I was, albeit at one remove, dealing with criminality.

In the event, it was both a disappointment and relief. He had turned himself in for unpaid fines.

Divorce is a big step for a family. While the idea might not have bothered Mr P—what might her children say about it? The answer came post haste. Vivian e-mailed me in May 2000:

> *Tina was worried about what her sons might think. She sat them down and spoke with them. Their reaction was very interesting. They thought that it was a good thing because it was the first good or smart thing Dad had done in a long time. I think Tina is doing a fine job with these boys on her own. Definitely better than if their Dad had stayed in the picture.*

Although Tina was no maverick, it was clear her husband was. I would be much happier when he was no longer an issue. It took what seemed like ages. The following month, Vivian again e-mailed me. The date of freedom for Tina was set for May 15, 2000. Once joined in holy matrimony, they were now in an odd piece of US legalese to be 'bifurcated', assured Vivian.

> *Tina says hello and wants you to know she has been diligent in trying to get these papers done. She is in awe at the box of medicines that have arrived at her house. She called asking how much goes where and how often. There are a lot of big needles that will be used daily for 3 months. She's OK now, just taken aback a little. Ta ta for now.*

There I was interfering in these people's lives. Lives that were very different from my own. Criminality, jail, bifurcation. What sort of maelstrom was I being sucked into? On and on the saga went. The papers were lost by the court. Then they were found. The summer was approaching. People were going on holiday. It felt as though nothing would ever happen. Then on 6 July 2000 the message came from Vivian's office, 'Vivian asked me to pass on some information to you. Tina's divorce papers went through and everything is done. A transfer is scheduled for next Thursday.' After weeks of inactivity, events were moving rapidly.

The relief was huge. I could feel my baby becoming more of a reality.

Vivian wrote a few days later: 'Edie did well. 11 is a great number. We'll have plenty for this x-fer and some to spare. Tina's uterine lining is nice and thick. We have a room booked for her at the Hilton on Mission Bay for Thursday and Friday night with a late checkout time on Saturday. She is taking off work until Monday. So far everything is looking very good and going as it should. On the 19th or 20th Tina will have the blood test that will indicate if you are expecting, have a bun in the oven, in a family way, etc.'

Everything was starting to happen.

Edie had delivered 19 eggs. Of these, 11 were fertilised. Eight continued to divide into embryos. I felt I had almost a football team and that maybe I should mourn the three that had failed to make it. In the meantime, my season had begun. More than 300 children were descending on me. I was now commuting from school to school with my office in my car. Sitting in one of the schools, I checked my e-mails on my laptop. In came a message from 'babiesplus' with an attachment 'embies.jpg'.

Another click. Four circular specks with fuzzy edges. My latent family. A frisson. This was real. Life went on. Children needed to be taught. The Course Tutor had failed to show. The teaching team needed to be re-jigged. I clicked the attachment shut, closed my laptop, put it in the car and drove off.

This was becoming my normality in the summer of 2000. The following Thursday found me at one of my schools where my 80 plus students for the summer were arriving from Heathrow Airport. I was in the office, bathed in dappled light through the leaded windows, overlooking the sunken gardens, taking in their passports, tickets and pocket money with all calls diverted to my mobile phone. A French girl was sitting in front of me when it rang. It was Dr Smotrich on the line.

'I have Tina on the speaker phone so she can hear what you're saying and you can talk to her. I am just about to implant four of the fertilised eggs in her.'

'Oh, good'.

(To the French girl 'May I have your passport and any French francs you would like us to keep safely until you go home?')

'How are you feeling, Tina?'

'Just great.'

'Let's hope something happens.'

I felt useless. What do you say when you are making

82

babies at one remove half way round the world in the presence of a foreign teenager you have never met before and who fortunately has no idea what a life-changing event is happening?

'Well, this is quite a moment.'

The girl smiled, thanked me and left. Coming to England was quite an event for her, but she did not and does not to this day know quite how dramatic that moment was.

I just had to wait until the 20th to see if anything had worked. It had. Dr Smotrich told me the test he did ascertained degrees of pregnancy. Tina was very pregnant. I could not imagine the difference between 'pregnant' and 'very pregnant'. I was soon to find out. I would also find out why Dr Smotrich had implanted four embryos. The beautiful Edie (who I later discovered was called Melissa, but I still know her as Edie) had proved popular with Vivian's clients. She had produced lots of eggs. Many had become fertilised, but what I had not been told was that no pregnancy had resulted. The man before me in the queue had had four implanted. No babies had resulted. The man after me had experienced the same. For me, it was beginner's luck. When Dr Smotrich phoned me, he told me I should sit down.

'It's three.'

'How does Tina feel about this?'

'She's shocked.'

'Surprised?'

'No. In shock.'

In implanting four with the hope of creating one, three had resulted. As to my own feelings, I was just delighted that there had been a result. The idea of three had not sunk in.

In a way I was relieved that it had not been four as then we might have had to think of removing one. Reduction had been a philosophical and euphemistic concept. It would have turned into a real and ugly consideration of whether to kill a child.

Few were in on the secret at that stage, but one friend I told said 'You can't have three. That's too many to manage.' 'OK. Which one do I kill?' That's what it came down to. That stopped any further discussion.

Never throughout her pregnancy had Tina raised with me the idea of reduction or expressed any regret at having gone ahead with so many. It was only when I thought we were in danger of losing them all that I had moments of doubt. Was it because we had been too selfish or squeamish in seeking to protect ourselves from the need to make a horrible decision that we were taking risks with these babies' lives?

Tina grew large at some speed. Within a few weeks she had to give up work. Because her maternity leave would be so long, her employment as a nurse was terminated. Her only income came from our arrangement. Technically, she was reimbursed for her expenses, but it ensured that she was not worse off than she had been.

I imagined that she would come over just after Christmas. I researched the hospitals that could cope with triplet delivery and put Dr Smotrich in touch with the nearest one. He seemed happy enough.

All was not well, however. Not well at all.

I had assumed everyone was delighted and wanted it to stay that way. At such a distance, I did not spot what was going wrong. The shift from joy to apprehension was fundamental and would threaten the entire plan.

It was Vivian who alerted me to Tina's unhappiness. Towards the end of September, she wrote, 'There are a lot issues coming up for Tina that we need to iron out. First keep in mind the tremendous amount of hormones she deals with. You've heard of how pregnant women are so emotional. It's true. Pregnant women can cry at the drop of a hat. Since Tina has three babies she has three times the hormones. She has been in quite a state since the pregnancy started. She didn't plan on being put on bed rest at all and then she is put on it almost immediately. If she doesn't return to work in 30 weeks her employer will not keep her job for her when she returns. She can reapply and they would hire her again but only if a position is available.'

Real problems, I felt helpless about what to do. Vivian went on:

'Then Dr. B. tells her that he is concerned about the medical attention she will receive in England. If she goes into labor or it's time for her c-section and there aren't enough beds at the hospital, where will she go and what will happen? Is she going to a NHS hospital or private? One of the most common problems for multiple pregnancies is that they haemorrhage because their uterus is so stretched. In which case she would require a blood transfusion. She wants to know if the blood in England is tested for diseases like it is here.'

Did Tina really think England was a third world country? There were practical concerns, too.

'When she comes to England will she and the boys be in a flat? She likes your home, but she is concerned about the boys being too disturbing to you and your father. Also she is allergic to the cats and allergies are always worse during a pregnancy. When we were there before she had to use her inhaler quite a bit.'

That was something I felt I could reassure her about.

At least Vivian struck a positive tone at the end, 'Before I go I have to tell you this. I asked if she was regretting becoming a surrogate mom. She said "No, not at all. It's all worth it and I think Ian will be very happy." She's great!'

That was true, but once again I felt that everything was going wrong. There was something else that lay behind all these fears. I had to find out what. Taking the bull by the horns, I called Tina.

'I think we can iron out all the practicalities, but what's the worry that underlies all this?'

'I'm afraid of dying. I'm afraid for my sons. I'm afraid of them and me being far from everyone we know. If my uterus ruptures, I have to be treated immediately, or I'll die.'

That was clear enough. It was a dreadful feeling. There I was seeing joy and delivery; there she was looking into the blackest chasm imaginable. I sensed desperation. She told me she would happily bring the babies over herself.

How could I square this circle. My first thought was a selfish one—to present to her the problems that would arise from the babies being born in the US. They would have to be granted entry here. They would be American. They would not have residence. If they were born here, they would *de facto* have residence and I might find it easier to get British nationality for them.

When I thought it through, my attitude was wrong. My first concern had to be and to be seen to be for the welfare of the mother and babies. That could not be compromised for the sake of making immigration easier. My way forward was clear. I wrote to Tina to tell her that we would do whatever she felt happiest with. The worries disappeared; the blood pressure steadied.

'Tina called me after you sent your letter,' Vivian emailed. 'She felt so much better. She had been so worried that she was going to upset or disappoint you. I was very happy to hear her relief. She is really doing very well considering the circumstances.'

It was clear that the babies would be born in San Diego. They would be little American citizens and I faced going through hoops to get them in and keep them here.

10

Three Sons

Throughout the pregnancy I felt detached and quite out of control, although Tina, Vivian and the medics did their best to keep me informed. The ultrasound photos from San Diego showed that I had fathered three small specks with appendages. These might have been a head, a hand, a foot.

Even the video they took of the babies on 9 November showed to my untutored eye, humanoid shapes swimming into and out of focus. How each baby could be repeatedly identified as 'A', 'B' or 'C', I had no idea.

How any guess could be made as to their gender, I could not imagine. Tina was confident. 'It's two girls and an unknown.' she told me in November. The doctor had looked. He was more circumspect when I spoke to him. 'We'll see if we can find a boy in there somewhere'. Tina was certain, though, that he had told her he had definitely seen two girls.

Vivian thought she had seen something male on the video. I was lost in admiration at her perception. I peered at the videoed pointer and saw nothing that resembled anything. Without anything else to occupy my thoughts, I was keen to know what was in store for me.

'We tried the pendulum test which is what I use to determine babies' sex,' she wrote. 'I haven't been wrong yet in predicting a baby's unknown sex. You might think this is fiddle faddle but it has not let me down yet. I'm betting on girl, girl, boy. You'll have to select so many names!'

So from November to February, I became adjusted to the idea of two girls and an unknown. To avoid any disappointment, I focussed only on what I knew. There were two girls. There might be three. I wondered if I would be disappointed at not having a son. I pushed any such thoughts away, although I knew that I secretly hoped that the unknown would be a boy. Over the weeks, I convinced myself that it was likely to be three girls.

Every time I thought of going through all this again on the off-chance that another pregnancy might result in a boy, I told myself this was a nonsense and that I really should rationalise what it is that makes most men want a son in their family. I must be thankful for the babies, no matter what their gender.

Nevertheless, I told Dr B. that a boy with two girls would be the icing on the cake. Vivian asked me to give a selection of names. I thought through all the possible permutations and e-mailed a list covering two girls and boy with which names were for the girl born first; three girls with the names for the first and second born; two boys and a girl and for three boys.

All eventualities were covered. I agonised over the two girls and a boy permutation. Tina loved my choices. The easy ones were for three boys. I knew they would not have to be used.

Focussing on theoretical names took my mind off the real issue. The end of 2000 was a fraught time. In December and again at the beginning of January, Tina had some strong contractions. They were controlled with medication. Things were going wrong.

As each hour ticked by, the babies' chance of survival increased. Every day the percentage chance rose. If they had been delivered in 2000, there was no more than a 50% chance. I was waiting for disaster to strike, relieved when the twentieth century ended and the twenty first began.

Tina was admitted into hospital for the duration as a precaution. As January slipped into February, the babies increased in weight and each day in the womb was a bonus. Their lungs were becoming stronger and Tina was invariably optimistic. When I received a photograph showing how big she had become, I could not believe a person could stretch so much. She was huge and refused to let her head be in the shot. Still, never in any of my conversations with her was there a single word of regret.

There was not so much as a word that maybe we should have reduced. I was not so sure. I had sailed into a high-risk pregnancy on a tide of humanitarian anti-abortion ideals.

By early February, Tina was unable to breathe lying down. The babies were compressing her lungs. She had to sleep sitting up. Even that made her breathless. The only emotion I was now feeling was one of guilt. All this was for me, yet I was carrying on with life as normal. None of this had impinged on my freedom to do so. This brave woman was in pain, separated from her home and family, unable to sleep properly, distended. There was only an acceptance of the situation. How would a 'maverick' surrogate have coped? How could I have been so fortunate?

By the afternoon of 8 February, time was running out. In a message headed 'ready to explode', Vivian wrote 'Tina can't take it anymore. For a while she was breathing fine, but now the babies have grown so much that there is no more room for her lungs. At this point she can't even lie down. Dr. B is away until Monday. I believe once he returns he will let Tina have a c-section. So in all likelihood you will officially be a Daddy next week.'

I phoned Tina. She was panting. 'Can't the doctor come in specially for you? You can't go on like this until Monday.'

She calmly assured me she was sure he would and that, even if he did not, there were others who could perform emergency surgery. When I woke up on the morning of 9 February, I found that Vivian had mailed me in the early hours. Her message read 'Delivering tonight! Going to the hospital now. Tina having contractions that won't quit... call you right after.'

At 9.15 I was in the kitchen with my father preparing his breakfast. He had wandered away from his chair, following me, when I answered the phone.

'Hi, Ian.'

This was it.

'You have…' and Vivian read out the list of boys' names that I had concocted so quickly with, for each one, the weight. Nowhere were there any of the girls' names I had carefully selected. Had I misheard?

'But that's three boys. No. Are you sure?'

'Oh yes. I've looked.'

'But where are the girls?'

'Yes, everyone got it all wrong.'

'You'd better bin that pendulum.'

'Yes, I shall.'

'Wow.' I clung to my father. 'Give my thanks to Tina.'

'OK'.

'Oh, when were they born? Our today was your yesterday. Were they born on the 9th, today, or yesterday, the 8th, your time?'

'22.00 or so on the 8th.'

There was nothing more to say. My father was in his own world. There was no one with whom to share this joy spontaneously. I rescued yesterday's paper from the recycling bin as a memento. The names did not ring true. I recalled the e-mail I had sent some weeks before and changed them: Piers, after 'Piers the Plowman', Ian after me (on the basis that the oldest is the oldest and the youngest is the youngest, while the one in the middle is just the one in the middle.) In my mailbox was a message from a former student, Lars, a Norwegian with whom I had kept in touch for years, telling me his wife was expecting. Serendipity again. I needed a third, short European name. Lars—the

Scandinavian for Lawrence. The list was complete. Middle names were easier. Thomas for Piers. That was my father's second name. Aidan for Ian. I just liked it. And 'the great I AM' appealed as initials. Conrad for Lars to continue the nordic theme.

Three boys. No girls. I had the icing, but not cake I had expected. This was reality. I had to accept the concept of three sons and what this entailed. Two concerns had vanished. No hanging around outside ladies' loos and no visits to the Fairy Shop in Marlborough.

'Aren't you disappointed?' said my father's social worker. 'I know you wanted to give one of them your mother's name.'

'I don't even think of disappointment,' I replied. 'I just accept.'

And I realised I meant it.

11

Nanny Knows Best

I phoned Tina every day following the birth.

'How are they?'

'Wonderful' was the invariable reply, the dreamy intonation expressing her contentment at the sight of the babies as well as pleasure in their progress.

I rather selfishly hoped the dreaded bonding was not starting. I wished I could hear a cry, a gurgle, something approximating real contact. A week and a half after the birth, it appeared I was not the only one who was noticing the lack of contact I had with the babies.

'The doctor wants to speak with you', Tina told me. 'He thinks you should come over and see how the babies are looked after so you know what to do. "Premies" aren't like normal babies, he says'.

Quite how different they were, I had no idea. Concerned, I contacted Vivian. I wondered why the doctor was so worried that he wanted me to fly out there so he could tell me how to look after the babies. A few things came to mind. Did he think that because

I hadn't appeared I must be uncaring and therefore unfit to have the babies released to me? Was there something wrong with them that I didn't know about and that he hadn't told Tina? Or was it the famous US fear of litigation—a fear so strong that he thought I would sue if some problem developed with them that could be put down to the hospital not having given me hands on training?

My huge worry was that under English Law the babies had no right of entry. None at all. US visitors are granted the privilege of entry which can, of course, be refused. A recent scandal about an internet adoption had made immigration officers more suspicious of babies coming in from the US. I wanted to try to sort out the legal side and, now that I had got my father into good physical condition, reduce the nursing home days to a minimum. I did not want him to return to his emaciated state, nor could I bear to think of him lying bleeding and urine-soaked in a home with me thousands of miles away, unable to act. I needed to make my visit brief.

I was getting quite twitchy that my status as a carer here would lead to my being assumed to be uncaring there. A year later on a breakfast TV programme, a prominent pro-life campaigner would accuse me of just that. 'Mail-order babies,' she called them. How that stung.

I wondered if I would really have to persuade the hospital to release them to my care. I asked Vivian to find out what the doctor's fears were so that I might try to allay them.

Vivian had her own ideas. 'I haven't spoken with

the doctor so I can't say for certain what the concern is. I'll bet it is the litigious aspect. We live in a very litigious state. It is the paediatrician's responsibility to be sure the babies can be cared for. However, anything you need to know he can tell you in the short time you are here. But of course I agree with you that you'll have no problem. It may be that old double standard again, you're a male, you aren't even allowed to select a cot. Tina and I have no doubts whatsoever in your abilities. Here is an angle. Tina is presently caring for the babies and being given all kinds of information. She can even take the preemie class offered at the hospital if she chooses. Since she is travelling back with you she can teach you anything you can't figure out and the doctor needn't worry. In the meantime I'll try to find out the doctor's true concern.'

Would the worst happen? Would it be the hospital I would have to fight to get the babies? Again my head was buzzing with all the worst case scenarios I could imagine.

Vivian was able to set my mind at rest. 'You have nothing to worry about. The doctor just wants to be sure you can manage. I think the only problem now is that he has no sense of who you are. As soon as you can talk with him I think he will feel reassured that everything is going to be all right. Nobody thinks that you do not care. Tina has told the doctor your predicament with your father, how you would like to be here but just can't yet. Also how she is completely confident in your caring ability. There is also nothing wrong with the boys. All he could say about them being discharged was "it will probably be a couple of weeks and they will probably not be discharged at exactly the same time." I know you are aching to see them and hold them but try to relax. We'll keep sending pictures and updates.'

That I wasn't to be allowed to select a cot was another instance of this assumption that males cannot care. I had phoned a local shop's baby department and asked for their advice about cribs versus cots and cots versus cot beds. I was being confused by choice. The woman at the other end of the phone asked me to bring my wife in. When I said I would come in, she said she would give me brochures to take home for her. I had lived with the idea of being mother and father for so long that I had forgotten that they were two people.

It was when I thought about a nanny that I realised I was out of my depth. At the time, the world-famous Norland Training College was just down the road. I phoned to ask if I could come in and talk to them.

'No need, we can do it over the phone.'

'Actually, I would rather speak to someone face-to-face. I'm only ten minutes away.'

'We can do everything over the phone.'

Clearly here was a business that had more customers than it needed. I revealed all over the phone to a disembodied voice who said she would put me on their news sheet and suggested I should not have all my eggs in one basket, so to speak, and that I should contact Newbury Nannies.

Newbury Nannies seemed more interested, not to say fascinated. Nevertheless, I was left with the impression that looking after a baby was an arcane practice to which only the professionals held the key. The ladies at my father's day care centre were more down-to-earth. 'You keep them clean, fed and provide some entertainment.' I felt much better.

Norland sent a nanny for interview. She was fully aware of my position. Norland had published it all. She came with a representative from Norland ostensibly to give her a lift from the station, but I am sure it was to check me out. We seemed to hit it off. The lady from Norland was supportive. That was the last I heard.

Newbury Nannies were more discreet. They asked if they could give my details to a maternity nurse. The interview was friendly enough, but she returned for a second visit. 'Why do you lock the doors upstairs?' she wanted to know. I had thought it was self-evident that with an elderly dementing person in the house, any room could be used as a loo and all contained hazards of some sort. I knew it would not be popular, but I had to say it. 'I'm sure you know about caring for babies, but I think you will learn something about caring for the elderly if you come here.' I was told that my father's room would have to become the nursery and that he would have to go elsewhere. I had already come to that conclusion, but I knew that, however gently it may be done, I was going to be bossed. We parted on good terms. She told the agency she would take the job, then thought the better of it and changed her mind. I was on my own again, but felt strangely relieved.

When it became clear that I would not have either

of the two interviewees living in my house, my thoughts turned to using an agency for non-resident night cover and involving people I knew for the other times. Meanwhile, I phoned the hospital every day to check on progress.

Tina was in there on a daily basis helping with the feeds. I spoke to the doctor who had wanted me to come over. His concern was that I should know about basic cardio-pulmonary resuscitation. We talked about how the babies were and there seemed to be basically no problems with them. During the first two weeks they took a couple of their three-hourly feeds from the bottle, but they did not always take everything in. Nevertheless in week two they achieved and exceeded their birth weights.

It was in week two that I heard Piers cry. It was the most direct contact I had with my children. I wanted to hold him. I told Tina 'If I come out for just a couple of days as the specialist wants, I just don't see how I could fly back here without them.' Tina's reply—'I know. That's how I would feel if they were my children'—was unconsciously reassuring in a double sense. As I thought, she did not see them as her own children. When we had touched on this before they were born, she had said 'I feel more like I'm baby-sitting than pregnant.'

It was at this time that I received the photographs in a 'brag book'—so called because parents can put it out and brag about their children. The three of them looked very much the same. At week two, Tina could tell them apart only because Piers and Lars had feed-ing tubes on different sides and Ian was smaller. 'His eyes are closer together', Tina said, 'but I think when his head gets to the same size as the others', he'll look like them.' So shocked had I been that they were all boys and so concerned with their well-being that this was the first time I had thought of how they might look. I might in time have to adjust to three very similar looking sons. Their improvement continued through week three.

Piers was progressing more rapidly and was taking all his feeds via the bottle. Ian was not far behind. Lars was some way behind them. My arrival day would depend on him. Just as soon as he got the message about sucking and learned how to suck and breathe simultaneously, he would start to make the same progress as his brothers. In the meantime, I knew that the costs were mounting.

12

Birthday Flights

Hospital costs had not featured prominently in my thinking at the outset. The baby—as I had been thinking in terms of just one—would be born in the UK. Part of the contract with Tina involved covering her uninsured, 'deductible' and 'co-pay' medical costs— whatever that meant. As soon as it became clear that the babies would not be born in the UK, I looked at the insurance cover I had taken out, just in case, with more than a little interest. It was impenetrable. US insurance-speak is incomprehensible to the untutored. Anyway, I knew I was covered.

I assumed that Tina was covered for her own medical expenses. I had heard of how astronomical US hospital expenses were and thought all Americans had insurance cover. I was sure we had talked about this and that she had told me she had it. I could hardly ask Tina about this now as she might feel under pressure.

As soon as she was admitted to hospital, they became interested in Tina's arrangements. Understandably, as she was busy contracting, she did not want to go into the details. I asked Vivian, out of curiosity, what the cost for the first week was. '20,000' was the brief e-mailed answer. I assumed dollars and held my breath. Paula, my US lawyer, confirmed that Tina's insurers had twice refused to pay on the grounds that the pregnancy was via surrogacy. She thought they might reconsider given the impetus of possible legal action. As surrogacy had not been specifically excluded from Tina's policy, I thought it was reasonable to assume that it was included, or at least that it was worth a legal challenge.

In the event, the hospital fees were proving to be the least of my problems. Left with debts by her now former husband, Tina had decided to time the bankruptcy she had been planning for just after the time she delivered. If the insurers would not pay up, she would simply include the bills from the hospital with all the other bills. I had not known about this.

Vivian thought Tina's medical costs would top $100,000 by the time she was out. I had to resist the thought that the sooner she gave birth, the better. At least the boys were covered by insurance.

Paula told me Tina was being a 'real trooper' and asked if I would cover the cost of looking after Tina's sons while she was in hospital. In fact, Tina and I had already spoken about her sons and I had agreed that, of course I was willing to pay for them to be looked after.

The moment the babies were born I set about getting them covered under my US insurance policy. I had become so used to doing everything by e-mail that I sent one to the insurers. The response was that I should tell my employer. I had a quiet word with myself and sent back the message that I was contacting them in my capacity as my employer.

Clearly this was something my correspondent had not been programmed to comprehend. I heard no more. Although Vivian, who was rapidly becoming my fount of all wisdom, assured me that American businesses only responded if there was a problem, I was not so sanguine.

My fears proved to be grounded. Tina told me the insurers had told the hospital that they had not got the babies on their books. As it was now 20 days after the delivery, I could see myself having to foot the bill for this period before the babies were covered. My fingers danced over the keyboard in faxing the insurers and sending copies of my e-mails to them. I also phoned their help number. I was told to contact the broker who had arranged cover in the first place. My call to him was met by an answering machine. So as not to lose more time, I faxed to tell them this and ask what more I could do to ensure cover. Their faxed response was reassuring. The babies were covered from '2.8'. I just hoped this was their birthday on 8 February and not 2 August.

The broker sent me an e-form to complete and fax back. I still did not understand the insurance details, though. With hundreds of thousands of dollars at stake, I felt I should. Despite being ostensibly written in English, a letter from the hospital about insurance was incomprehensible. My broker nonetheless gave me some hope that costs would be within bounds. He ended, 'Good luck!' I felt I needed it.

Although I had managed to convince myself for the first month that the babies were, in a way, still to be born even though they were outside the womb, by the fifth week this rationale was less credible. I was feeling pangs of longing.

I seriously considered flying out to take them back one at a time. The logistics were insurmountable. For every one I brought back, there was one I had to leave behind to get another. The only practical solution was to wait until Lars was released, had been photographed and had his passport. I would have to continue to be pragmatic and push my parental urges to one side.

My daily calls to the hospital continued until the first week in March. Ian and Piers were likely to be discharged soon as they were feeding themselves. Lars was more laid back and let the tube do some of the work. The specialist was cagey about estimating when they would be ready for travelling. But I needed a date, a goal, and knew it would be me who fixed it.

I had to balance between rushing to see them and hold them and letting the hospital have time enough to consider them fit to travel. A quick visit to the internet showed that flights to San Diego were filling three weeks beforehand. Arbitrarily, I decided to travel on my birthday. This would be the day that I would see my children and it would become a sort of alternative birthday for all of us. I allowed a few days after that in case the last one had not been discharged and booked the return flight for the babies, Tina, Tina's two sons, Vivian and me, for 27 March. I had checked with BA earlier about how they deal with very young babies. Each baby had to be attached to an adult for take-off and landing. Three babies: three adults.

Tina thought it would be a 'closure' for her sons to come over and see the babies in their new home. They had never flown or been out of the country. As a new-comer to jet-setting, she was ill-at-ease at the thought of travelling without Vivian, who was to be the 'logical' third adult. Vivian was willing to come and her husband was happy to take over the business for the duration. Eight tickets. I confirmed the bookings. The date was now fixed. 23 March. My fingers would remain crossed.

The problems continued. The very next day, the specialist told me Piers would not be released. He had apnea. This meant that his heart rate dropped when he was feeding and, more significantly, when he was sleeping.

His monitoring needed to be continued. Both he and Lars had low blood pressure. The doctor opined that a blood transfusion might be needed. He was cautious and unhurried. The flight dates did not seem like such a good idea now. Although he told me that all this was to be expected with premature babies, I had little else to do but fret.

The District Nurse in Newbury confirmed that babies had very low blood pressure and that apnea mattresses were available. Was it that the doctor was concerned about air pressure in flight? This seemed to be the case, whether because of any real danger or the fear of litigation in case the side of caution was not erred upon, I could only speculate. Two days later

Piers was out. The hospital had pressure on bed space. The caution had disappeared. Patients had to be processed.

After another day, Lars was out, too. They were on monitors and Tina knew what she was doing, but these little boys would have to take their chance away from the hospital's cocoon. This was a business very much like any other.

13

Nice Cup of Tea

There is an established procedure for most aspects of life. Often in Britain it is prefaced with 'have a nice cup of tea.' Does one tell friends before or after the event that, as a single man, one is having a baby or two or three? How to explain it? Does it need to be explained?

Without any existing set of behavioural norms, I had to draw up my own. Before the birth, I decided to tell those who I thought would have been saddened not to have been taken into my confidence. I had to bear in mind the legal advice not to say anything to anyone and had to apply the strictest precautions. I tried it out first on my employee-to-be. He should, I felt, know what changes there would be in my household before he took on the job.

The next step was to formulate a rationale. It should be brief, factual, unlikely to shock, bore or titillate, to explain events and elicit the desired reaction to them. The analysis concentrated my mind and reduced to the essentials why I was doing what I was doing in the way I was doing it.

In the years I had spent toying with the idea, the reasoning had become so convoluted that I had forgotten where it had started. First I had to reduce the element of angst.

The refreshing difference between Growing Generations and Surrogate Family Program was the elimination of any angst-inducing angles. The load of baggage should be lightened. I tried a synopsis:

When I realised most of my life had been as a carer, I also understood why it had taken the shape it had and why the normal events in life, such as marriage and family, hadn't happened. As it could carry on like this for a while longer, I thought I should do something about it before I became too old. I could have joined an agency, met people, married and had a family. All this takes time and chance would be a fine thing. Carers don't get out very often. In any case, to marry for the sake of having children is a bad basis for a relationship. I would have to marry someone far younger than me. Children might not happen for a long time, if at all. I would just be getting older. Even if there were children, it might be that the relationship would break down. I could see a failed marriage, hurt feelings, bitterness, recrimination, divorce, emotional scarring, loss of custody, house, business. It could all be such a disaster. Far better to think though logically what I wanted—a family—and how to achieve it. So I went to an agency, found a surrogate who for various reasons liked being pregnant and the kudos that surrogacy could bring to an otherwise ordinary life, found an egg donor who combined attractiveness with an excellent health record and a masters degree, located a specialist IVF clinic and created a family.

* * *

What I had lived with for so long sounded so simple, so straightforward, that I imagined the only reaction would be 'Oh. Right then.' And, indeed, with almost everyone close to me, this is what happened after the jaw-dropping shock had worn off.

There were some surprising reactions, though. One of my ex-employees asked 'If you need to give love, aren't your cats enough?' A married woman who long ago decided against children ran from the room. So brief was my analysis and so protracted had been media coverage of other family creations from the US that the concepts became confused. 'So you'll bring them here when you've adopted them, then?' 'But will they let you adopt them?' It took a while before the realisation that they were biologically mine set in.

When the babies were born, I set about choosing Godparents. Each boy was to have his own—two Godfathers and one Godmother. I decided to take advantage of my international connections. Lars had Lars. Ian had Ian. Piers could have had a Piers, but I had not seen the only Piers I knew for years.

One of the first people in on the secret was Esther Rantzen. I talked it through with her as a friend. Her husband, Desmond Wilcox, was more than a little interested. A documentary was mooted. Over lunch he reinterpreted my reasoning. He saw the logic.

'You're clever and courageous,' he told me. 'I'm sure you have the ability to change the minds of the vast majority of people in this country towards surrogacy.'

'But you tackle really interesting subjects, like 'The Boy David'. That one really tugged at the heartstrings.'

'So would this. Believe me.' His eyes penetrated my indecision. I attempted to persist, though.

'It all seems so boringly logical to me that I can't see how it could be sufficiently interesting material for a documentary.'

Having admired Desmond's work, and knowing that when he said he would film just what I found acceptable, nothing more, and that I could see him as a sort of honorary Godparent, I could believe him. I knew I had nothing to fear from it. In the end, my conclusion was right, although my deduction may not have been.

We spoke some time later. 'It's been done to death, they tell me. They look at the gays and that's that for surrogacy as a documentary topic. I tell them they're wrong, that this is a quite different angle, to believe in my intuition, but I just can't get anyone to produce it.' In a way it was a relief. I would not have to make a decision that my children could have regretted. As I believed so strongly in the moral rightness of what I was doing and took the view that others in my position would find it liberating, I was saddened that, if such a luminary as Desmond could not find a backer, this story and all that might flow from it would remain hidden. Within six months, Desmond had died and I had met the real 'Boy David' at his memorial service.

I assumed that the story would never be told.

My UK solicitor, did not share my willingness to reveal my children's history. He advised caution, feeling that whatever one did could be twisted round and turned into something unrecognisable at the hands of the tabloid press. Publicity was to be avoided—certainly before the children were in the UK. I asked Esther. She had little doubt that it was a 'story'.

'Come on my programme. Tell your story. You can be in disguise.'

'Why? I have nothing to be ashamed of. Even so I don't feel the need to defend what I have done.'

'It goes against the grain as a journalist, but I would advise that the best way to deal with any publicity is to say 'wait for the book'. I've read enough of your letters to know you can write. So write a book.'

It had not occurred to me. She was right, of course. Even if it were never published, it would be remarkable record for the children. I liked the idea. If nothing else, it would give me something to occupy my mind while I was waiting to go to the US and collect the children.

With so much information, I took an eclectic approach. Memories were starting to fade. As the reality of the children drew closer, I found I was quite happy to forget the convolutions surrounding their creation. I knew that when they were here, I would have thoughts only for the future. The computer enabled me to be scatterbrained. I put down the memories that were likely to disappear first. The early setbacks had been so depressing that I wanted to forget them. Down they went onto the hard drive in random order. How could Jane Austen have had the intellectual discipline to start at the beginning and proceed until she reached the end all in longhand? My admiration for her knew no bounds.

14

Panic... Even More Panic

As the date for my first sight of my sons approached, more hurdles appeared. The hospital had told Tina that Piers and Lars needed to be connected to apnea monitors, but that the insurance company would not allow their machines to be taken out of the US. I would have to buy them at $4000 each. Also, I should check with the airline as some of them do not allow apnea monitors on board and would not take babies who needed them.

Would I ever get my sons out of the US? I asked the Health Visitorn at the local surgery about apnea monitors. Yes, I could be supplied with two machines on loan. Now for British Airways.

I picked up the phone. The BA clerk was Scots. 'I wonder if I could set an anxious mother's mind at rest. I would like to take two babies on a flight, but they are used to being connected to a baby monitor, you know the sort that sends out a warning that is supposed to prevent cot death. Mothercare does a roaring trade in baby alarms.'

'What's the monitor called?'

'An apnea monitor.'

'I'll check.'

Had I made it sound casual enough?

'What sort of batteries does the monitor use?'

'Not sure. Ordinary batteries, I think.'

'If they're the sort you can buy in the shops, like Durex, that'll be all right.'

Not sure you mean Durex, but they'll run on Duracell.'

There was a hint of embarrassed amusement.

'Is there something wrong with the babies?'

'No, it's just a precaution.'

The Health Visitor confirmed that the monitors would, indeed, run on Duracell batteries. One hurdle cleared.

The other was a reappearance of an earlier sticking point that I thought had been sorted out. Tina's hospital fees. The subject had not been mentioned since Tina's first week in hospital. The e-mail from the lawyer was terse.

'I talked to Tina recently and she has expressed concern about the mounting medical bills that she is receiving. I assume that Vivian is in contact with you about this issue as it is her responsibility to keep you fully informed. I understand that you have insurance for the babies and that this policy is covering the bulk of their medical costs. When all of Tina's bills come in they will run in excess of $100,000.'

It was another aspect to worry about. Was this the language barrier coming into effect? Just when I had thought something had been resolved, it was seemingly back in the melting pot. It had all appeared clear to me, but had the bankruptcy been abandoned? The US medical expenses were something I certainly hadn't allowed for.

Going bankrupt is not to be taken lightly, at least in the UK. Maybe this, like so much else, was different in the US. I did not feel like telling the lawyer that Tina's bankruptcy was what I wanted, partly as it was not, but mainly because I had no wish to be seen to know about it. I assumed this was what Tina wanted to do in any case to clear her own debts and asked Vivian that very question. 'Oh, yes' was the response.

But another message from my lawyer with another crisis came hard on its heels. The US bankruptcy laws were to change in the next few days.

'I spoke with Tina and stressed the urgency of getting her bankruptcy petition filed tomorrow. She is in a panic because the forms are very long and require detailed information. I have also spoken to Vivian and told her that she needs to clear her calendar to help Tina with the babies.'

'I am perfectly happy for Vivian to look after my babies,' I emailed back, 'Tina and Vivian have been wonderful throughout and I trust them totally.'

Along came another hiccup. Tina wanted one of the doctor's bills to be paid in full. As I have always paid my bills, I concurred and sent payment. However, no one can be singled out for settlement in a bankruptcy, so this doctor was not paid in full. He felt aggrieved and contacted me.

Separated by a common language and communicating in cyberspace, I felt the distance between us was a distorting mirror. Was I right in sensing an unwelcome change in the atmosphere? I imagined Tina buried beneath bankruptcy papers.

'Will they be with you?' I asked Vivian. 'Have you cleared your diary?'

'No need. I just looked after the babies for an hour or two while Tina saw her lawyer.'

There was no hint of panic or rush. Considering the amount of money at stake, not to mention the welfare of three tiny children, there was an Alice-In-Wonderland quality about the messages I was getting from America. There was panic and there was no panic. Something had been agreed and suddenly seemed not to have been agreed before being relegated to having been agreed. Was this how it would be when I was with the babies or was it just because of the distance and language? There was nothing else to do but count the moments until the babies were safely in the UK and I regained a modicum of control over my life.

* * *

The day before I left, my solicitor had arranged a three-cornered telephone meeting with an immigration specialist. They painted a bleak picture. Coming back with Tina was not a good idea, he thought.

It was at this point that she and the babies could be refused entry and deported. I was to try to distance myself from her and her sons and go through the EU channel carrying, somehow, the three babies and a pile of supporting evidence. If I were waved through, I had to declare that I wanted permanent settlement for the children. I had to be upfront and state the full circumstances.

Both legal specialists advised me to delay my trip and apply for a visa from the British Consulate in Los Angeles. However, having paid for eight transatlantic tickets, arranged a brief stay for my father in a nursing home and organised a sitter for the house and cats for the duration, I was unwilling to change my plans and apply for a visa which might be stalled by red tape. I also wanted at last to have the babies in my care. Tina had done a brilliant job, but it was time for both of us to pick up the threads of our lives and move on. I would take a chance with Immigration at Gatwick.

I was told what papers I would need. I would have to prove my paternity. I phoned Dr Smotrich and asked for a statement of this. 'Ian Mucklejohn is the father.' It needed to be clearer. I phoned again and a clearer statement of my role in the fertilisation came over the fax machine. 'Ian Mucklejohn's sperm was used to fertilise the enbryos.'

I had to prove that I had suitable females to care for the babies. Newbury Nannies organised a day nanny in addition to the maternity nurse already arranged and faxed confirmation. I had to prove that I could afford to bring up three children. I had to ask my accountant to supply the latest company accounts and tax returns. I had to arrange for my house to be valued and for the valuation to be faxed to me in America so I could present it at Immigration. I had to bring my latest bank statements. All this during the afternoon before my flight. All this because I was a man coming in with my own, provably my own, children. It was demeaning and illogical. A clear case of the law being an ass.

* * *

The QC's opinion faxed to me that afternoon raised the question that the local authority would judge whether I was suitable to have my own children live with me.

He referred pointedly to the Kilshaw case which had been making headlines a few years earlier and that had ended disastrously. In that case a couple from Wales had adopted twins from Missouri after outbidding by over $6000 the US couple that had originally taken the girls in for $5900. After saying to the US family she wanted to see her baby one more time, the mother handed them over to the Kilshaws who adopted them in Arkansas where adoption rules are relaxed. When their genetic father and the earlier family claimed custody, a British judge decided that the twins should be returned to Missouri to have a court decide who should raise them.

Although a case totally different from my own, it had, however, focussed attention on the difference between American attitudes and our own tightly regulated system and portrayed the former's contractual arrangements as being casual to the point of laxity wherein anything might go wrong and quite possibly would. I would have to live with the suspicion the Kilshaw case had caused. 'If public authorities do become involved... Mr Mucklejohn would be ill-advised to have his case tainted by any perceived illegality or deception in bringing the children in to the UK.'

While I was taking advantage of the liberal Californian approach to surrogacy as opposed to the (for me, at least) impossible English system, I could see no connection whatever between the Kilshaws' adoption and my own case. The boys were without a shadow of a doubt my children.

He thought there might be a problem authorising medical care for my own children. Without a residence order or other clarification of the legal position, as an unmarried father, I would not have parental responsibility Though he added 'the point is unlikely to be taken in an emergency and I am told that Mr Mucklejohn's' GP is aware of the situation and sympathetically supportive.'

I would deal with this if the occasion arose. As I had never had trouble authorising medical care for my students, I was quite confident about my ability to deal with such eventuality for my own children.

Most significantly (and ominously), the QC added, 'I have no doubt that when (rather than if) social services turn their attention to the novel situation raised by this case, their initial appraisal will be critical and searching. To avert unwanted state interference, Mr Mucklejohn needs to make careful and appropriate arrangements to provide a reliable and high standard of care both himself and with qualified assistance. Agency Norland nannies are, in my view, not quite enough especially as they are to be engaged at night. I suggest that further consideration needs to be given to the structure of the new family. I suspect that committed and available family help from a sister or cousin with family experience who lives locally will make a strong positive impression, if they are available.'

Sister? Cousin living locally? There weren't any. Effectively, according to his opinion of the law, the local authority could quite easily take my children away from me.

I thought of the many children already on the 'authority's' lists; neglected children who roamed the streets late at night; children at risk and could not imagine that anyone in authority, anyone with any sense, would follow this line of thought. Nevertheless, I would have to ensure that I would not be seen as the main carer in order not to fall foul of the law.

In case the local authority would want to consider taking care proceedings, the QC (who used the word 'when') added that 'the appropriate response will probably be a cross-application for a residence order. a possible resolution may be a residence order coupled with a supervision order in favour of the local authority for a limited period.'

So I would be put on probation. My own children would be taken in the care of this amorphous 'local authority' who might license them back to me.

I had an early warning about the media, too: 'This is potentially an extremely attractive story for tabloids and broadsheets.... The press can be expected to run it from a questioning and even hostile angle... I am certain that Mr Mucklejohn would be ill-advised to take any initiative whatsoever to use the press to support any application to the Home Office.'

It had never even occurred to me to do so. I had no desire for my private arrangements to be spread across the pages of newspapers. Compared to the earlier case, I did not see mine as much of a story really. But in a few months I would see how the press could add some embroidery to make it one. Tiny children, the elderly, the truth—all of these and anything else could be sacrificed on the altar of tabloid circulation.

A quick e-mailed query from the immigration specialist about the chance of an immediate visa were I to arrive in Los Angeles and request one had elicited a dispiriting response.

'I spoke to the Consul... As it stands the children have no right of abode in the UK. Nationality for these children is derived from the birth mother and [they are] not entitled to British Nationality. Please do not hesitate to contact me should you require further information. Please contact this office.'

My boys had no right to live in the UK. No right to be British. I was on my own. Legal thunder clouds were gathering as I began my journey. I had known for months that I had few rights to the children. It now seemed that my children could simply be taken away at any moment by the authorities as they mulled things over.

15

The Work of an Angel

And there was more. From the day the babies were born, I knew that there was something else that could go so terribly wrong that I could not even contemplate the ramifications. Although Tina had signed away her rights to them, this document, legally binding in the US, had no validity whatsoever in English law. She was the mother. She had all the rights. If there were a change of heart, everything would have to be argued out in America and there the babies would remain. I had absolutely no reason to believe that this would happen and it flew in the face of all the evidence, but it was a worst-case scenario that had preyed on my mind and against which I had guarded myself. Until the babies were in my home, in my care, I could not give way to my feelings for them; could not yet bring myself to consider them mine.

Vivian collected me at the airport in her green station wagon the smell of which reminded me of my visit to Los Angeles several lifetimes before. We drove to where Tina lived in El Cajon.

I was very, very apprehensive. By UK standards, it was a reasonable area with only the presence of a couple of 'Immigration Police' cars opposite Tina's block suggesting a darker side to the community. The apartment was small and cheek-by-jowl with others sharing communal paths and a small grassy area. It was a warm March evening. All the windows were open with a different TV station emanating from each. Two cots and a pram took over most of Tina's living room. The rest was occupied by a sybaritic couch that snaked round the room and provided the family's life-support centre with hinged flaps concealing the TV controls. The TV remained on constantly. It dominated life there. All conversation was to its background. Its huge screen demanded to be acknowledged with a glance every few seconds.

I was presented with a birthday cake. What a kind thought. I had forgotten what the day was. There they were. Three little people. I looked from one to the other. They looked the same. They were—babies. I could see a few differences when they were pointed out, but if their order were changed, I had to look for Lars's bald spot where a feed tube had rubbed away his hair, had to compare Ian's eyes with his brothers'. The one remaining was Piers by default. I felt I had created three little people, but after such a time at such a distance, they did not seem to be mine. Under Tina's roof, they were Tina's. Her sons told me what to do. I was the outsider who had come to take them away. I felt curiously detached. I recollected the pot in Santa Monica.

'Yup! Haven't they grown?' said Vivian. The tension broken, we laughed.

My Goddaughter, Josie, came down from Sacramento with her mother. I hadn't seen them for years. We went out for lunch. Without thinking it through, I had left the babies with Tina. She found it thoughtless, although was too considerate to tell me so. She was quite right. I had a family. I had responsibilities. I did not have the freedom of a single man. I needed to learn a lesson or two. I would have to do better. We sat in the shade of a palm tree out of the fierce March sun and took photos. I looked at the babies. They were out of context. I was out of context. It was all so incongruous. Exhaustion took over.

The hotel reeked of American plastic. Memories again. I collapsed into bed at 19.00 and was up at 01.00 each morning of my stay. By the time Vivian's husband, Claude, came to collect me to bring me to Tina's, I had already watched three movies and was ready for lunch. I sat with the babies and changed them, fed them and burped them. I observed Tina's sons' pet snake in its glass case make small writhing movements. I empathised. In spite of the bright sunshine, I felt depressed. I was jet-lagged in a foreign land and just wanted to get them safe home.

A telephone conference with London at 5 in the morning while I was in the San Diego hotel provided me with last-minute instructions. I was to organise my papers into sections, each in a plastic wallet. I was to keep copies. I was to be prepared to defend my right to my own children in front of an Immigration Officer at Gatwick Airport. It was an encounter I was not relishing.

There was another complication. All the passports had arrived, bar one. Lars's passport was missing. Vivian phoned the passport agency at 6.30 on the morning before the return flight. There had been an error and Lars's passport would be sent. Not wishing to take a chance, we asked to collect it and were told it would be waiting in the Federal Building in Los Angeles. Claude drove me. Three hours later in the carpool lane for two or more we were sailing past queues of motorised monsters containing one person. I dwelt briefly on the waste of resources, but had to concentrate on finding 11,000 Wilshire. Again that boulevard with the missing letter loomed into my life.

At 9.00 we were in front of the massive building in which lay an envelope for me. There was no way we could gain entry without an appointment. 'Can I speak to someone? I need only to collect an envelope.'

'Not without an appointment,'

'Can I speak to someone to arrange an appointment?'

'No, you have to phone for one. Here's the number.' I went to a payphone outside the building to phone to get in. It was an automated system. After pressing buttons according to instructions, I was allocated an appointment the following day, too late to travel. The armed guard told me to come back for the appointment. Further requests to speak to someone led to my being given a card with a phone number on it for enquiries. I tried the number from a call box. 'You can't call enquiries from a pay phone', the guard informed me when I told him of my lack of success. Vivian volunteered help from her office phone, but the promised return calls to my mobile did not materialise.

Corralled round the building without protection from the wind or sun snaked a queue of jaded would-be travellers. All had tales to tell of delays and expense. I found myself trembling with rage, impotent in the face of a blind bureaucracy that looked likely to frustrate all my plans. I joined the queue. Four and a half hours later, seemingly on a whim, the guard let in a few without asking for an appointment number. A notice board inside the hall invited comments and suggestions on the service provided by the Passport Agency to its Director, Tom Reid. Five hours after arriving, I left clutching the passport. I spent that night advising Mr Reid by letter on the apology for a service his Agency provided. His eventual response was to agree to pay Tina $105.

* * *

I had wondered about a meeting with 'Edie'. As her real name had been scratched out of any paperwork I had been sent, I felt she intended to remain incognito. I was happy with that. It seemed uncomplicated. Nevertheless, the children would eventually ask what their biological mother was like.

It had been my intention to describe to them her role in the process as that of a blood or organ donor. One is terribly grateful for the life-saving donation, but one does not knock on their door and maintain a lasting relationship. What if I really did not like her? What if she had personality traits that I found offensive? Would I be looking out for these in the children?

It was safer, in a way, to remain in ignorance. I had seen Tina as the mother, but now that I had to think for them too, I decided that I at least had to try and get in touch. 'Edie' had been 'open to a meeting'. It had been arranged for the day I spent kicking my heels outside the Federal Building, so I thought I had missed my opportunity. Luckily she was available on the day we left and I waited for her with Claude outside a café at a San Diego shopping mall.

What do you say when you meet your children's mother for the first time? Of all the odd things I had done, I thought this would be the oddest.

In fact, it was one of the most pleasant. Melissa proved to be delightful in every way. She told me about her ambitions to remain at the university as a post-graduate, her interest in languages, her own background, her travel to England and her English grandmother—and why she was content for her progeny to exist away from her knowledge and influence.

'My mom left when I was two. My dad brought me up. I have never seen her as my mom because she never did the job. That's why I don't see myself as the parent of these children. I'm not doing the job.'

It was beautifully logical and, although it interpreted 'parent' in a narrow context, it was an argument that I could live with. There was no anguish; no area for doubt. This beautiful, articulate and intelligent woman saw what she had done as purely transactional.

I could see no aspect of Melissa that I would regret seeing in the boys. We posed side by side, looking slightly awkward while Claude took my camera and clicked the shutter.

There we were. What was likely to be our only meeting was preserved; frozen in time. I was utterly relieved and delighted that it had taken place. She felt the same, it seems.

In an e-mail to Vivian she wrote, 'It was so nice to meet Ian today. I was very impressed with him and I think he is going to be a great daddy for those boys. You know, I had forgotten that you told me they were boys. I was thinking the triplets were all girls! I want to commend you for making people's dreams come true. It was moving to see Ian so enthusiastic. Keep up the good work—it's the work of an angel!'

Angels have feet of clay, though. I had been immensely lucky. At various stages the babies could have died or been born handicapped. There could have been a huge case with the insurers. Tina could have decided to keep the children and lean on me for child support. The possibilities for disaster were legion. Not so much an angel as a lady who is willing to take a chance to give people what they think they want, I thought. I could not sleep at night in such a risky business. Vivian was serene. She was troubled by no such soul-searching.

Lars, Piers and Ian having a laugh at their father

Sitting pretty for the moment

Ian and his godmother

Piers lost in thoughts, cheek to cheek with his godmother

On one of their first days at nursery

Ian, Ian and Piers, and Esther with her godchild Lars

The babies in their Motherware buggy, pushed by Ian's students

Lars' drawing of his brothers and he, Valentine's day 2005

16

Home

I was delighted to leave San Diego. I heard my pulse as I walked down the narrow walkway, past passport control, through the perfunctory pre-9/11 security and stepped off American soil. No one had rushed forward at the last moment brandishing an envelope with a bill for hundreds of thousands of dollars. No one had barricaded the way, refusing to let these three little American boys leave.

My calm was studied and practised. I was in a turmoil that lifted only when I stepped into 747.

Even being on the BA flight was like coming home, although I hoped the constant questioning from strangers would not be a foretaste of what was to come.

I discovered that travelling with triplet babies is like carrying a huge sign 'Ask me anything you wish, no matter how intrusive, direct or personal'. We had the undivided attention of the female crew members. They were too professional to ask who the mother was and how they had been conceived. Not so the female American passengers.

'How were they delivered?' 'Did you have any fertility treatment to conceive them?'

I suppose Tina and I looked an odd couple. She, large and loudly dressed in an all-American way. I, slight, jacket and tie, discreet—in preparation for my encounter with the officials at Immigration. The babies were good travellers. Mindful of the ordeal in store, I popped a sleeping pill and, with their permission, left it to the ladies to feed and swab across the Atlantic. Tina's children were happy enough with their electronic push buttons and video screens.

I asked the BA crew if they could help me with the babies through the EU channel while the Americans went with the other aliens. In the event, BA regulations that prevented them from carrying a baby resulted in us all reaching the EU channel together.

I looked at the waiting passengers. Which were the journalists? Where were the cameras? Who had a tape recorder secreted in his coat? They just stood waiting in a line like the bored, tired travellers they were.

I had rehearsed my speech. 'I should like to apply for settlement for my children, please.' The EU clerk pointed like an automaton towards the aliens channel. 'I don't have the necessary stamps', she advised. The seven of us presented ourselves in front of an Immigration Officer who knew he had drawn the short straw.

The response to my question was 'Why did you not get a visa for them before arrival?' 'I didn't have the time. I needed to be back on the 28th as I'm full-time carer for my father and his placement at a nursing home ends today. "I have all the papers here describing the way the children were conceived, how I can afford to look after them and what I am worth.'

He glanced towards Vivian and Tina. 'Is one of them the mother?'

'The surrogate mother. Yes. She has her children with her. They are all on return tickets and will be leaving on Monday.' The officer disappeared. Now was the moment. Tina, her children and the babies could legitimately be refused entry. If I passed this point it would all become far more difficult for the authorities. But here was an alien woman with alien children who did not have to be accorded entry. It could all unravel in the next few minutes and I would have no redress. This was also the time one of the other passengers could turn out to be a journalist and splash the story across the front pages.

My throat tightened. The moment passed. It was all a welcome anticlimax. The immigration officer returned, asked for the passports and birth certificates to copy and gave the boys two month visas so I could apply to the Home Office. He wrote the address down for me. We walked out of the building. It was as simple as that. Or was it?

Bringing Tina and her sons over with Vivian may have been a practical solution and given them the 'closure' she wanted, but I sensed impending doom while they were in my house. Tina's role changed suddenly.

From being the main carer for the babies, she became a mere passive onlooker as other women took over. They greeted her briefly and took the babies into their charge. I made dinner for Tina's sons mainly in an effort to get them to sit down. As if I were invisible, they slid across the polished floors, imitated the way I said 'tomato sauce' and made real and imaginary farting noises throughout dinner. Vivian told me that after an hour of this, Tina was in tears in her bedroom and could hardly wait to leave.

Whatever the reasoning, our two worlds were colliding and I desperately wanted to part on good terms. Without any input from me Tina made it easy and resolved to book into a B & B near Bristol the next day to see Stonehenge. They looked into the nursery to bid farewell to the babies and left in tears. 'They'll be fine' was my instinctive reaction. 'So that's why they cried as soon as they saw me?' was Tina's. Vivian assured me that the family's tears lasted as far as halfway into the train journey and that the babies were not spoken of again. It was not difficult to envisage how my original plan of having Tina and her sons with me during the pregnancy would have fared—the stress would have been unbearable. Certainly she did me the greatest favour by staying in California. I shuddered at the thought of what results the tension might have had on the hazardous gestation.

The babies safely in their nursery, I needed to apply to the Home Office for 'Indefinite Leave to Remain'. It was a humiliating procedure. On advice, I had to supply a justification, a statement of my means and the following:

*v Statement from Dr Smotrich of La Jolla IVF that
  the children were conceived with my sperm*
v Statement from my GP that the children were moni-

tored and detailing their current health

- v *Statement from West Berkshire Social Services that I am the carer for my father*
- v *Statement from broker of share holdings*
- v *Land Certificate relating to my house*
- v *House valuation*
- v *Company bank statements for last three months*
- v *Personal bank statements for last three months*
- v *Payslips for last three months*
- v *Company accounts 2000*
- v *Company brochures 2000 and 2001*
- v *My passport*
- v *Piers's passport and birth certificate*
- v *Ians' passport and birth certificate*
- v *Lars's passport and birth certificate*
- v *Judgement declaring the existence of parental relationships and awarding custody*
- v *Letter from the Nanny Agency showing care arrangements*

Phoning, researching and writing dominated my first week with my children. Everything was posted on 9 April 2001.

I waited.

* * *

In the meantime, there were babies to bring up. My UK lawyers and QC's opinion had made it clear that there had to be nannies and that they had to be female. Now that there were three babies, there appeared to even more need for nannies —round the clock. For fear of having them taken away, I could not even leave an hour without nanny cover. A night-time maternity nurse and a day-time nanny took over the children.

Nannying became a ritual performed by those who knew what was what and I could only look on.

They were good. There was no denying that. I looked and learned—about timed feeds, about sterilising bottles, mixing feeds, how to operate the nappy disposal bin, but I felt an intruder in the nursery. I had come to believe what the lawyers had been telling me—that Social Services would expect there to be competent women to feed, change and nurture.

As for me, so far as the authorities were concerned, I was an irrelevance. I fetched and carried, assembled baby chairs from kits, provided a water filter, cleaned the kettle and busied myself with mundane tasks. The babies carried on being babies and I assumed the role of a man who left almost everything to women who knew best.

17

Mary Poppins

Nannies all have their peculiarities. I tried to adapt. I realised quickly that if you have two nannies in a room at the same time they are likely to come to blows, so idiosyncratic are the ways of their trade. Nanny A would cut the nails, only to be told off by nanny B who bit them. Nanny A would then get huffy and, behind her back, belittle nanny B's feeding routine. The type of bottle, the type of teat, the brand of milk—all were open to discussion. One nanny would want large, angled bottles, the other was happy with the straight variety that had come from America. As long as I had only one at a time, the nanny would get on with the job of nurturing and the babies readily responded to each of them. I tried to make sure each had her equipment of choice.

When the babies had become adjusted to a feeding routine, the maternity nurse made way for a regular nanny. She had her own way of working. The boys thrived on it, but I am not sure I did. I was further relegated to being a bystander.

'Not like that,' was the reaction to my bottle-holding. She preferred to communicate in writing. I would receive my instructions in list form and ticked off what I had obtained.

On the occasions that she spoke, I found I was dealing with a language in which the words used did not mean what they said. After little Ian had been operated on for a hernia, I was told, 'His scrotum's gone completely black.' I phoned the surgeon on the spot and made an appointment to go to see him in Oxford that day. I then took a look to see the tiniest trace of a small grey bruise less than half the size of my fingernail.

Later, when he lost weight between one health visit and the next, I was told, 'He isn't sucking. If he doesn't drink, he can't eat or he'll get constipated. If he doesn't eat, he won't be able to carry on like this.' Rather than steel myself against his imminent demise, I paid a visit to the GP. 'Put anything he'll take into him. If he's constipated, we'll deal with it when it happens.'

Having seen 'Mary Poppins', I thought I knew about nannies. Not so. 'Watch Me Play Daddy' was written on the case of a surprise video one nanny gave me at Christmas. The surprise was the absence of a comma in front of the noun. 'But I'm really a daddy, not playing at it,' I told her.

Retitled in my head as 'Watch Me Play, Daddy', I was able to do just that. What was fascinating was not so much the videoed toddling at playgroup, but the banality of the background soundtrack of nanny-to-nanny dialogue which by its continuous insistency seemed the main purpose of the activity. The tots just got on with being tots. I wondered if, a year or so on, my sons would have personal experience of the same vacuity of conversation.

Nannies have their own inner lives which they fortunately cannot communicate to their charges. I was soon made aware that some have maternal feelings that are given sharpened focus in the absence of an actual mother; feelings that transcend logic and in which the nanny becomes the substitute mother while the actual father is either dismissed as an inconvenience or resented as an intruder.

One of them, who told me she loved my sons as much as her own children, seemed to enjoy being with them all the time. In fact, she was lonely and unhappy, setting me up as the reason for her woes.

Her replacement told me with some relish that her predecessor's vilification had been so thorough that I had become a hate figure at the Twins' Club. I also gathered that neighbours had been given the benefit of this woman's appraisal of my character. How terrible it was that the children had never had a mother. How terrible I was to leave things to a nanny. I wondered why she had taken the job in the first place. I had always been completely frank about the situation and it was not as if she had suddenly discovered my single status.

It was when she wrote to tell me I did not know how close she had been to handing in her notice over a request I had made that was so trivial that I had forgotten all about it that I decided to end the nonsense.

Up to this point, I had just got on with my life.

Now I was being judged. It was a new and odd feeling.

But the lawyers had told me a nanny was a prerequisite to getting settlement from the Home Office, so I persisted in having one. I would just have to remain out of favour with the Twins' Club. Fortunately, I appointed two reliable and uncomplicated nannies—one for weekdays and one for weekends.

Later one of the 'Esther' programme's audience told me that the babies would be distressed at having different people feeding and changing them. I never saw them being other than contentedly responsive to whoever was busy with them. There was also the fact that I remained the constant presence in their lives. They smiled and wriggled when they heard my voice. They knew who I was all right.

And how I longed for the time when I could do everything for them on my own. It would come. But until they were officially mine, I would have to defer to the nannies. At least the two who became the regulars also knew how to relate to a grown-up. I was happy to feed, to play and to be the constant presence that I knew these little ones needed.

No one from Social Services visited. The Health Visitor and the GP came from time to time. All was well and I began to wonder what all the panic had been about. The babies were looked after and were doing fine. For all the notice the authorities took, I could have been bringing them up on my own.

Although I had no legal rights, not even the right to authorise an operation, I simply went ahead as though I had all the rights. So far as the hernia operation was concerned, I dealt with the John Radcliffe Hospital in Oxford and no one raised any questions. All of them visited the Children's Clinic locally. Never was my authority queried. They acquired NHS numbers and 'red books'. It was just as if they were UK citizens.

The Royal Berkshire Hospital once sent me a letter asking how long they had been in the country. I did not respond. Their follow-up letter was easy to answer. It told me the hospital understood that I was a visitor to the country and queried my date of entry and purpose of visit. I was delighted to respond to this one. I heard nothing more.

Time went by with nothing from the Home Office. I had to travel overseas for a day on business. I needed my passport and on 12 September 2001 faxed a request for its return even though this might mean going to the back of the queue. I could not keep my life on hold.

18

Informed Judgements

All through that spring and summer, I had expected press interest. There was none. Life was eerily quiet. My Courses came and went. The children were out and about in their triplet pushchair. Neighbours and friends visited. The babies were much cuddled and cooed over by my foreign children at the schools.

Without shouting the details from the rooftops, I made no particular secret of their background. No one expressed any objections. It no longer entered my head that anyone could be other than delighted at this happy family or that it might arouse any public interest whosoever. My application for 'leave to remain' was with the Home Office. I thought, or probably wished to think, that any newsworthiness must have disappeared by now.

How wrong I was.

* * *

Just after lunch on Friday 7 September 2001, I had a call.

'This is Social Services. I gather you are trying to adopt three babies.'

'No, I'm not.'

'Foster them, then.'

'No. I have three of my own.'

'Well, that's not for me, then.'

'Who are you?' I asked. I thought I heard 'Suzanne.' 1471 yielded 'the caller withheld their number.' A call to the local Social Services revealed that no Suzanne or Susan worked there. My mind raced.

The press? Maybe. Surely they would not pass themselves off as Social Services. Maybe it was some Social Services central unit. I was beginning to forget about it when, at exactly the same time the following week, the doorbell rang and my assistant answered. He invited the visitor in.

'Hello, I'm Susie Boniface of the *Daily Mail*. We are doing an article on surrogacy and issues regarding citizenship. We have heard that you have three children by surrogacy and would like to interview you.' Pause. 'Well, let me put it this way, if we have the information, you can be sure that the Sunday tabloids will have it, too. If you talk to us now, you can have copy control. You can tell me to sod off, if you wish.'

'I would never be so rude,' I answered, thanked her and took her card.

As soon as I closed the door, the calm façade fell away. 'Information', 'tabloids'—all this was new to me. So far, the anticipation had been vague; unthreatening. The reality that my little ones and I were to become a tabloid story was a bombshell. The story was breaking and I still did not have settlement.

I may have closed the door on this reporter, but something unstoppable and undoubtedly unpleasant was happening and I was supposed to make a contribution to it. I had no experience of tabloid newspapers; never read them. I just thought of them dealing in sensation. I didn't see my family as sensational in any way. I could not imagine how we could be presented as such. I was soon to find out.

I phoned a friend with experience in this field. She said, 'As your unpaid media advisor, and any advice is as good as what you pay for it, I can tell you that you could do worse than the *Mail.* The trouble if you make it exclusive, though, is that if any of the other papers want information and they can't get it from you, they get it elsewhere.'

'Or make it up,' I added. 'OK, I think it's clear, I'll get her back and talk to her.'

Susie Boniface took notes in shorthand. I found I was giving just factual answers to her questions. They were mainly of the 'when, how and why' variety.

'So what control do I have?'

'I'll read you back my notes, if you like.'

'OK, I thought that would be all. I'll get my assistant in.'

We listened and made some brief corrections. Her snapper was at a local pub and responded at once to her phone call. I presented an existing photo of us all rather than have the babies presented for photographing. I was photographed sitting in the garden and idly lounging on the lawn—a somewhat unaccustomed pose for me. An hour later, she phoned back and asked the value of my house.

Informed Judgements

'What do you want this for?'

'So our readers can make informed judgements.'

* * *

Just before midnight on Sunday 16 September 2001, I had a brief foretaste of what that meant.

'Are you the Ian Mucklejohn in the *Daily Mail*?'

'You have the advantage. I have no idea what's in the *Daily Mail*.'

'You are and the story about the baby deal.'

'You've just woken me up. Do you know what the time is?'

'About 11 pm?'

'It's almost midnight. You'll forgive me for saying that I find this unacceptably intrusive.'

'Sorry. Can we call you in the morning?'

'I'm at the optician.'

'When's that?'

'Look, you've woken me up, I'm not thinking straight. Just phone me and take your chance.'

I went straight to the computer. Nothing on the *Mail*'s web site. What would be in the story? I was seething, tired, anxious and unable to sleep for hours.

I awoke the next morning exhausted and red-eyed. My gate was blocked by a silver car. Trapped. Must be the press. What on earth do they want? Is this what it's going to be like? In fact it was Susie Boniface clutching a copy of that day's *Daily Mail*. She offered to be a minder and, in return for an exclusive arrangement whereby I would talk to no one else, she would undertake that the *Daily Mail* would run an article on any subject I wished. She knew that the care of the elderly was close to my heart. While we were talking, she saw me getting my father ready for breakfast, feeding him and preparing him for day care.

'If I agree just to talk to you, the rest of the pack will think there's something to hide. They'll talk to people around me or just make it up. That's not what I want. I've nothing to hide. I think I should be able to talk to anyone.'

'You'll have everyone on your phone.'

'I'll take my chance, but thanks anyway.'

She expressed interest in having someone see what I was doing with my father.

'He's not an animal in a zoo.'

She talked about care and left when I agreed to her suggestion that a writer should come and interview me about this subject the following day. In hindsight, I was naïve to go along with this, but care for elderly was a subject I would very happily talk about.

'We're not out to get you. I have done people over, but only when they deserved it. You don't deserve it.'

That was reassuring. I told her my father was away by 10 in the morning and that I could be available then,

Within an hour or two, I had been approached by TV stations, papers, magazines and radio stations over the phone and in person. When the last satellite van had left the road; when the last photographer and TV journalist had removed themselves from my house; when I thought I could get back to my life, a radio station in Melbourne, Australia called. By ten to nine that night I was in a radio discussion with them. By nine I had turned off my phone system. They might want me to do a lunchtime programme in New Zealand. They could want. I was off to bed.

The questions had all been the same. Some had expressed themselves more tactfully than others. They ranged from the urbane Stuart Norval's 'Why, Ian, did you work so hard to achieve this?' to Radio Berkshire's 'So you think that if you've got the money you can buy babies?' Most were in-between. Sally Taylor of 'South Today' responded with a 'So that's what you wanted, but what's best for the children?' assuming an incongruity. Difficult to respond with the hearing aid in my ear providing a time lag to her question and an echo of my previous response, while I had only the camera's black rectangular eye to focus on. A news agency in Bristol wrote 'I would really like to write a piece on how you recently took the very brave and groundbreaking steps towards purchasing triplets over the internet.' It was really quite easy to decline their offer.

In the middle of the mayhem, West Berkshire Council phoned to tell me that, as the *Daily Mail* had revealed a 'large office' in my home, they would be requesting business tax.

'Actually, that's my sitting room. Don't believe all you read in the newspapers.'

Nevertheless the Council sent in their inspector who, confronted by sofas and a coffee table, had to agree with me. The alacrity of this department to squeeze money from me was impressive. It was good to know though that their colleagues down the corridor in the Social Services department must have felt comforted by what they read, for they didn't call.

David Rendel, my local MP did call. He offered whatever help he could with the Home Office. He thought it was daft that they hadn't given a decision before this and thought a nudge from him might help. I thought I would stick to the rules, wait for the six months to be up and then take him up on his offer. But by the next day, I had changed my mind. My own passport had still not arrived and the Home Office was clearly going to sit on it for a while. I phoned David Rendel and asked him to intervene. His secretary called back to tell me they needed the request for my passport in writing. I told her it had already been faxed and posted. She told me I could expect to wait another three months for the file to be dealt with, but that I should get my passport back shortly. It was nice to have a helping hand among the chaos.

It was on the morning of Tuesday 18 September that the doorbell rang at a quarter to ten. I was making breakfast for my father. A tall, white-haired woman in black had arrived in a Mercedes estate car.

'I'm Mary.' she said brightly, offering her hand. I shook it.

'Mary?' I assumed a surname would be volunteered.

'Mary Riddell.'

I thought I might have heard the name before.

'I'm sorry I'm early.'

'I'm just getting my father ready for day care. We're in the kitchen. Come through.'

He finished his yoghourt and milk, I removed his apron, put his shoes on, tied his tie and put a dimple in it and then helped him on with his jacket. Mary Riddell twittered approval at what I was doing.

'I think it's important he goes out looking as he would have wished to look before all this.'

Her agreement was immediate; her praise for my work fulsome. I took my father out to the taxi and then told her I would 'Just change out of my getting-father-into-the-shower-and-getting-wet clothes.' She and my assistant went into the room that had been my previous assistant's office. He made coffee for her and chatted.

Mary Riddell was charm personified. She was eager to ask about my father's condition. She was sympathetic and sensitive; warm and friendly. I told her what had happened when I was eight and how the diagnosis six years before had helped me accept full responsibility for looking after him. When I assumed that the interview had finished, she asked me, as in passing, questions about my life; my feelings for the babies; relationships I had had. I asked her about her own children. I chatted quite freely, although I could not see its relevance to my father. I was surprised when she wanted to photograph the children. I told her I did not want any newspapers to photograph them, but that she could copy one of my pictures.

'Do you want to see them?' It seemed the polite thing to offer. She had come all the way from London.

'Oh, yes, if I may.'

I took her to the nursery. She approved of the look of the babies. I felt had been with her long enough.

Off she went to be followed by a writer from another tabloid. I had forgotten about her. This one seemed particularly interested in the Godparents. This was not such a friendly chat over coffee. The questions were pointed; the questioner insistent. I told her I would not tell her who they were. The interview was not long, but she wanted to wait for a photographer and hung around for an hour or so while I got on with things.

How trusting I was! I should never have given either of them the time of day. This was when I thought that it was right just to tell the truth. I learned quickly that the truth can be spun so far that it becomes something else entirely. That something else was about to hit me like a physical blow.

It was an Irish radio programme on Friday 21 September that alerted me to what had happened. It was my last day of media innocence. A charming female brogue had almost persuaded me some days before to talk to Gerry Ryan on his phone-in show. She had spent nearly half an hour telling me how wonderful what I had done was and that her 67 year-old father had provided her with a 6-week-old sister.

'No, it's you women who are the lucky ones,' I had said.

'No, no!' she assured me. 'You men can father children whenever you want. Look at Picasso, he was 87.'

'Oh, yes, and have the press come back on me for creating orphans? No thanks.'

'But you don't have a biological timebomb inside you.'

* * *

On the Friday, the same voice rang to ask if I would do the following Tuesday—and added 'wasn't it a dreadful article in the *Mail*, accusing you of controlling the babies like a business and even condemning you for getting cots and clothes in Mothercare? To be sure, where else would you go for them?' Well, maybe there was no 'to be sure', but it sounded like it.

'Why do people have to write such things? You were doing something so good.'

I was taken by surprise. I hadn't seen any article. And then it dawned on me what had happened. I cancelled arrangements with Irish Radio and drove to the newsagent.

The article was venomous. I could hardly recognise myself. It was like being done over in the playground by the school bully—nice to your face, but destructive afterwards. My boys were spread across two pages with horrible words all around them. 'Made to order', 'Just bought three babies', 'How can he think he'll make a good father', 'Controversy'. This was a totally new experience. Why would anyone want to do this to us? Nasty it certainly was. Nevertheless, it also had a ludicrous side. Having adjusted to the shock, I tried to see it for the fictional imaginative prose it was.

Mary Riddell clearly had a thing about cleanliness. My house was too clean. My tables were unsmeared. It had escaped her needling eye that my little babies were not even at the crawling stage, so how could they provide the smearing she thought so integral to a happy family home?

And 'he has even been to Mothercare for cots and clothes' was there, as had faithfully been relayed by the

Irish Radio researcher. It was preceded by 'He had organised his new life as clinically as a corporate acquisition'. I laughed. Are fathers off-bounds at Mothercare? Or was her implication that it would have been more groovy if they slept in nappies on the floor for a while—a bit like middle-management on a survival course perhaps—till I finally got round to finding an acceptable store.

The world of the tabloids is rooted in an idyllized golden-age '50s when life was simpler, gentler and no one locked their doors. That they did not lock their doors because most people had so little there was nothing to steal does not fit this image and is ignored. It is the fundamental honesty of the '50s that shines through instead. Theirs is a world in which all suburbs are leafy, all drives are gravelled and all families are nuclear. In this view single-parent families are of course still anathema, rather than a fact of life for a large number of children raised in this country.

I felt vulnerable and sad to know that this was journalism in the twenty first century.

It wasn't just the fact that it was me they were attacking. That I could just about live with. It was the fact that my babies were being objectified, as if their existence didn't matter enough to make some cheap points. There was no way they could respond to this verbal lashing. I had unwittingly been placed in a situation where I had not been able to protect them.

19

The Legs of a Story

No more random interviews, I decided. Just Esther, of course, and maybe one that the BBC's Religious Affairs department had spoken to me about—half an hour, one to one, face to face, non-confrontational interviews about those who had had life-changing experiences and the moral and ethical issues involved. Everything else had to go. And I wanted to see no new people. I was retreating in on myself. It was horrible. I phoned Esther.

'What a complete hatchet job.'

'No, not a complete hatchet job, just a hatchet job. I wouldn't let Mary Riddell over my threshold.'

'I rather wish I hadn't.'

'Look, don't go taking to strange writers without running them past me first.'

* * *

But it isn't that easy to turn off the media. I received another call from the reporter of the tabloid who had been so interested in the Godparents.

She phoned to say she had been buying water locally and that someone had told her Esther Rantzen was
one of the Godparents. 'Did you think that choosing
a high profile person like Esther with her connections
to Childline to be a Godparent would help you get residence for the babies?' I could, of course, have
answered simply 'no' and should have done. Instead, I
repeated that we had known each other for years.

Within the hour Esther phoned me with a list of
questions they had given her, inviting her to justify
surrogacy, my sons, me and her status as 'patron' (sic)
of Childline. We discussed the line to take.

'It's a private matter. To say anything is likely to give
the story legs.'

'OK, I'll say the same.'

A while later she told me she had answered the
questions and, as she had been libelled by that publi-
cation twelve years earlier, had insisted that her
answers be taped. I would have to learn from her.

The article was a long time coming. On 11
November, it appeared over two inside pages. Once
again almost every 'fact' was wrong. There was none
of the rhetorical questioning of the *Mail* that had carried a certain believability with it. This was pure fic-
tion. Here readers were instructed how to react. The
babies were to be christened in their 'costly gowns'.
The *Mail's* Mothercare clothing had been promoted to
'designer-label clothes'. The fact that that their photograph be taken became 'Ian was reluctant to kiss or
cuddle the boys as he posed for photos and seemed
uncertain how to hold them.' In fact, the one that

adorned the article was one of my own copied from the *Mail*.

It all just added to the remarkable picture the writer was painting. I had become 'TV Esther's Tycoon Pal'. There was 'shock' expressed that she was to be god-mother. The source of the shock was unspecified. That was the only part that had not already been reported with generally more accuracy in other papers and, no doubt, the reason this freelance writer's work was finally given the light of day.

Readers were invited to contact a 'Triplet Hotline' at the paper with their views. My poised fingers twitched with anticipation at doing just that. What was the point? I had already been hung out to dry.

David Mellor, former MP and Minister fallen from grace because of a sex scandal, weighed in as well in his 'Man of the People' column, decrying 'designer babies for spoilt millionaires'. As I changed my father's incontinence pad, 'spoilt' was not an adjective that sprang to my mind. Nanny, who was helping me with the children, ribbed me without mercy and made me do the washing up. Even tycoons have to do the chores sometimes.

29

Juice and Bananas

I had suddenly become a public figure. Yet my fifteen minutes of fame were unwanted. It was an odd feeling. I had never thought about anonymity before. Took it for granted. Had never valued it. But I did now. The *Mail* had presented me for judgement by the British public. Other newspapers had carried the story almost verbatim over much of the English-speaking world. There I was: there were my sons: all of us had become public property. Just a story. Yet I was the same. A human being. My children were innocent little babies. They, too, were being presented—for what? Entertainment? Pity? They were more than a diversion. They were real little people who deserved better. We were private people no longer.

Who could have done this to us? The factual material in the original *Mail* article could only have come from America. No one in the UK knew the name of my American lawyer. Only a few people there knew this and all of these were bound by ethical codes of confidentiality. Someone in America had made money out of this at our expense. I would love to know who. It could be anyone and this suspicion, sadly, has served to cloud my relationships there.

I thought people might believe what had been written about us. In this, too, I was wrong. In the middle of the media attention came personal messages from people I had never met. The British public were great. I received only wonderful letters. A woman e-mailed me her photo with her toddler by her side. Another sent prayers, followed by a large parcel containing three hefty storybooks, twelve cassettes and a perfumed purple card.

Messages came from across the world. 'Kerry' in Australia wrote to me at 'Beverley Hills', Newbury, England (the *Mail* had told its readers this is what the locals call the area I live in). At least the Post Office knew where it was. She told me: 'I would have patted you on the back for having the courage to do what you did. I have four beautiful children and believe you will have many, many smiles. Thank you for reminding me how lucky I am. Congratulations on doing something as beautiful and creative as fathering your boys.'

Another came from South Africa: 'I have just finished reading about you in one of our local weekly magazines and I feel completely and utterly compelled to tell you how I feel. Your story is one of remarkable courage and initiative, and I salute you for your decision to have your sons come into the world in the manner that you did. I feel uplifted and inspired by your bravery and your initiative.'

Even the *Mail* forwarded one: 'I have spent most of today wondering if I should write this letter. I am not even sure if it will be sent it on to you. However, I just want to say how moved I was by your feature in yesterday's paper. To be honest, I did read the article initially with some cynicism but just looking at the photo made me realise what a wonderful decision you made and how genuine you must be, not only in looking after your new sons but your father, too.'

Another, from Eire, passed on by GMTV ended 'You made my day.' That one made mine.

Maybe after a while I would send them all a note. For the moment, I was smarting from having been made aware so brutally of the difference between appearance and reality. I saw 'journalist' behind every approach.

I took a rain check on the several lunch invitations that came by e-mail, phone and letter. A rain-checked caller phoned me again while I was working late at night. My reaction revealed in every way how I felt.

'I'm sorry, I can't deal with anything new and don't want to meet anyone I don't know. I'm trying to get my life back together and feel it's been intruded on enough.'

'But I want to be a plus, not a minus.'

All I could see was a complication and a nuisance. I was getting as tetchy as the *Mail* article maintained.

'I'm sorry, I just need to have some quiet, so I'm going to wish you goodnight.'

I replaced the receiver. It rang again.

'I just wanted to write.'

'Well, go ahead.'

'I haven't got an address.'

'It's in the book.'

A day before I would never have been so abrupt. I knew I was changing and that it might not be for the better. She wrote a letter with a photograph and a number for me to call; a number, she said, that only I knew. I feared a stalker. I started closing the blinds at night.

The following week, I had fewer calls. I declined Irish Radio and German and Danish TV. The only pre-arranged encounter was with the BBC's Religious Affairs department. I thought they would be unlikely to give me a journalistic mugging. Two delightful ladies came—Christine and Belinda. I was inordinately suspicious.

They wanted to assure me that the series they were making—'Life changing TV'—was not confrontational, was concerned with the moral and ethical issues that guided people in choices they made in life and that it was to do with ordinary people in extraordinary situations. It was a phrase Desmond Wilcox had used.

They also assured me that the material would be handled with sensitivity and that the object was to get people to tell in their own words about the choices they had made and why they had made them. The viewing audience would be left to make up their own minds on the points raised. The only point that seemed to me to be an issue was personality.

'We would like you as a person to come through, so the audience can gain an impression of you through your interests.'

'Such as if I collect stamps?' That was not what they meant, of course, but through it I might understand what they were after.

I had never had to justify myself or create an impression before. Carer, organiser, teacher, postman, bookkeeper, father. I'm not sure I really have much idea where the 'me' part of me fits into all this. When I was a child I used to get through two books—often a Rider Haggard and a Dr Dolittle—on a Sunday morning. I was quite serious-minded and had a developed sense of responsibility; an awareness of right and wrong.

This was exactly, the ladies said, what they wanted. This would give the audience a sense of who I was as a person. The stamp collection need not be revealed. Here was the real me, for better or worse. The two ladies left the decision with me.

Before the shock of the previous week, I would have loved to do the programme. Now, the last thing I wanted was to have a repeat performance. With them, I felt I was among friends, but that feeling was coming from a couple of complete strangers.

* * *

The letters continued to arrive. All were positive. Most wanted to meet me and have something to do with my family. I suppose 'you look nice' and 'you seem to be a nice, brave, admirable person' should be quite flattering. Some appeared innocuous: 'Your story impressed me so much. I would be thrilled if you would keep me informed of your progress.'

One was tempting: 'I would LOVE to be granny to your boys. I want to cuddle them and nurture them and say to you that I think what you have done is absolutely right. My own grandmother was a source of unequalled love....'

For once, my response was positive. But I asked people in the media about the granny and, sure enough, she was a freelance writer. I cancelled. The e-mailed response was rapid. She had bought presents prior to her visit: 'I'm thinking to send them to you with love and the price tags on, then if you see fit you can reimburse me.'

I decided not to respond to anyone. No one seemed to be contacting me for our benefit. They all wanted a piece of me and my family for one reason or another. How I appreciated my life as it had been— just my family and me. What a pity the story had been broken.

In the middle of all this, my father's health took a turn for the worse. His heartbeat was described by a doctor as 'unsustainably slow'. It was the word 'unsustainable' that I had to act on. He was in the North Hampshire Hospital the same day. The consultant was informative. His heart was slowing and would, in a few months, stop.

Generally, they would fit a pacemaker under local anaesthetic. In my father's case, this was difficult as he would lash out at the surgeon. A general anaesthetic would kill him, so it would have to be sedation. Even so, the procedure could go wrong and he might die. Only if the quality of his life would be improved, would the consultant recommend the operation.

I deliberated. He had become immobile, needing both arms held to be able to walk. His speech had become garbled. A slowing down of the flow of blood to the brain could, I was told, increase confusion and physical disability. Maybe this was a cause of the deterioration. The consultant and I decided to go ahead.

I took him to the Brompton Hospital in London and the operation was performed on 27 September 2001. When I collected him the next day, I had a different father. This one was friendly, appreciative and capable of conversation. I hoped the change would last.

In any case, he had survived the procedure. We drove back through the Friday evening rush hour traffic in golden sunshine. As it was the second anniversary of my mother's death, we stopped at Chieveley churchyard to place flowers from the garden on her grave before taking my father to a home for some days' convalescence with trained staff on hand. The driving had been a break from what was becoming a routine.

On my return, the cards from people wanting to meet me and e-mails from the media were waiting to be opened. I replied to none of them.

But a critic there was—albeit not to my face. Nanny came back from playgroup one day in November to tell me what had happened. With some glee, she told me 'We got someone chucked out!' 'What happened?' 'A lady came in with her toddler, came up to us and played with us. She asked me if we were the children from the paper. She told me she completely disagreed with what this father had done and said she didn't understand how I could work for him. I told her that her opinion was her own affair and didn't count with me. She then disagreed with everything I was doing, like my giving the boys their juice and bananas. The lady who runs the playgroup asked if this lady was hassling me. I said I didn't want the boys hearing what she was saying, even though they couldn't understand. So the lady in charge told the woman it was her prerogative to decide who came and who didn't come. She grabbed her child and left without comment to me. She was told never to come back.'

And then I heard from the Home Office.

21

The Home Office

The Home Office wanted confirmation of what I had already told them and proved in documents I had sent them. 'Are you British? How did you acquire this nationality? Were you born or adopted in the UK or were you registered or naturalised as a British Citizen in the UK or were you born abroad and acquired your nationality by descent by virtue of your father's British Citizenship?'

I took this to be 'How British are you? Are you quite British, British or very British?' I hoped that my birth certificate would tell that I was as British as could be, so I copied it and sent it off. They also wanted to know that my name was entered on the children's birth certificates as their father. Odd as the Home Office had the birth certificates in their possession.

The other burning question was about Tina's marital status at the time of birth. Had she been married or separated, I would have had to state the nationality of her husband. As she had been 'bifurcated', I was able to state this. They required evidence. I wrote to her for a copy of her divorce papers.

The letter finished with 'given the area with which we are dealing it may take some time before our enquiries can be completed.'

It still seemed quite simple to me. They are my children; Tina is not related to them; here they are, here they stay.

Yet the law, I knew, was far more complex. What was unimaginable a few decades ago and certainly at the time many of the laws were formulated, had become a fact around which it had to bend its head.

The QC I had consulted had pointed out the anomalies in my situation. He stated in his opinion it 'would seem to constitute clear discrimination on the grounds of sex'. But when the 1981 British Nationality Act was passed, it was justified on the basis that 'it was difficult to prove paternity' at the time.

Developments in modern technology and in particular DNA fingerprinting had since made it a great deal easier to prove such paternity. But until Parliament updated the law, the only challenge to it was via the provisions of the European Convention on Human Rights on the 'right to respect for private and family life' and the 'prohibition of discrimination'.

This challenge of course was against a ruling that the boys wouldn't receive permanent leave to remain in the country, that is to say they would be extradited. The QC opined that a challenge would only be successful in my case, subject to there being 'a female relative resident in the household willing to look after the child and capable of doing so.' With my aunt in her nineties living a hundred miles away, this wasn't going to be a winning proposition.

Curiously, for the gay couple, the decision had been made within a couple of months. They had just breezed in. Their surrogate was, I gathered, married. Their children were happily settled in this country.

Though undoubtedly my sons' father, I seemed to be fair game—as I was to discover on the 'Esther' programme.

'It's about whether dads can be mums,' the driver told me on the way to the White City for the recording.

Sitting next to me on the podium was a British surrogate, pregnant and well-versed in media-handling. Next to her were two men casually dressed. One had been dropped into lone fatherhood by bereavement; the other by divorce. They had coped brilliantly with the task that had been thrust upon them.

Not for them were there any probing questions inviting them to justify their existence. Some decades back it might have been different. One could only sympathise and admire.

Having just watched the previous, rather upbeat programme being recorded, I thought I would try a casual approach. One of the audience, an agony aunt, launched the attack. 'When one has a disabled child, one compensates. You have created disabled children. They will have no idea of the interplay between men and women.'

Another followed up 'You cannot always have what you want. You have manipulated events.' A buttoned-up matron at the front, skirt clutched tight around her lest some contagion might seep osmotically from me to her, considered I was unworthy to be on the same podium as the other men and was in it for 'self-aggrandisement' as I had admitted to being on the programme three or four times before. It seemed to make no difference that I had been on the programme over several years on completely unrelated issues. There was no stopping her.

Esther phoned me the following day. 'I think I'm the only one who knows how sensitive you are. You cover it up so well. That woman in the front was very cruel. I think she's 'pro life' or something. You could have said, "Do you know how hurtful what you have said is?"'

'Actually, I thought at the time, what I wanted to say was that she would feel much better after a good rogering and that, had I not come on the show out of loyalty to you, I wouldn't have had to give people like her the time of day. But I suspect you would have edited it out anyway.'

'We have to cut some time, so I'll see what we should edit out.'

There was my private life and my private persona and, by my very presence, there was I inviting these people I would never see again to have a poke around in both.

Another woman in the audience had seemed to have taken a leaf out the Jeremy Paxman charm hand-book.

'You don't even know that you'll be allowed to keep them, do you?'

I could think of better ways of spending a Wednesday afternoon.

'I think these women saw you as a threat,' Esther told me. 'There you are proving you don't need a woman in your life. You can just get on with things. What you have never made much of is what you do for your father.'

'Of course not. I know how he would feel about how he is now. He would hate it and he would hate everyone to know.'

I knew that she was saying it stopped people knowing what I am really like, but I felt that the guard was what was holding me together.

22

Upstaged

I realised that the next journalistic opportunity for the tabloids to use my children to increase their circulation would be the Christening. This was scheduled for 18 November 2001. I was attending Bible Classes in preparation for it. 'Now—if you can—and don't feel put on the spot—but if you feel you can—and I shall quite understand if you cannot—but if you feel you wish to share this with us—can you say in just two words what God means to you?' In the presence of so many of the faithful, I had to acknowledge my own lack of conviction.

'Oh God (if there is a God) save me (if there is salvation.)'

The invitations had been dispatched. Replies were coming in. There would be more than 100 guests and nine Godparents.

A reporter whose story had not then appeared phoned to ask if she could come. 'It's a pity that the story wasn't in the paper,' she said jauntily, expecting me to agree that it was a shame that my private life had not been blazoned across the nation's breakfast tables yet again. Sensing my reaction in my silence, she continued, 'The Christening is coming up and this means we can approach the story from this angle. We would like to be there to take photographs and run the story.'

I was on my best behaviour. 'Thank you for asking, but no I shall decline.' I also resisted the offer to reconsider my decision.

Unversed as I was then in the ways of the newspaper business, it came as a surprise to find that the taxi driver who took my father to day care had been offered £500 by the same reporter to tell her the date of the Christening. There might be uninvited guests.

I apologised in advance to the two couples whose babies were to be Christened at the same service. £500 for a date that had already been published in a tabloid and a venue that had been stated in the local rag.

How much would they offer for a tasty piece of gossip? How much for a fabricated allegation? A few days later I discovered that the price for this was £15,000. That was what the taxi driver told me the reporter had offered him.

The local newspaper phoned wanting to take a photo at the Christening, telling me Church office had told them the BBC would be there. That was news to me. It was news to the Church office. I declined this offer, too.

The Christening was a real event. We had a Godparents' dinner the night before at The Dew Pond, a beautiful little restaurant near Watership Down. Everyone stayed in a small guest house in

Newbury. Ian and his little daughter, Alice 'aged 6½', stayed in my house. After the meal, we sat where we had sat two years before and reminisced on all that had happened in the meantime.

My father's taxi driver took the boys and me to the church in his Mercedes. Esther had just arrived at my house and followed with nanny and Ian. The Mercedes drove onto the paved entrance to St Nicolas' Church. A flash bulb exploded. Esther helped get the babies out of the car. Another flash.

A bevy of photographers was waiting outside the church gate. Jonathan Aitken, disgraced former government minister who was reading for a degree in Theology at Oxford, had just finished taking a service there and I wondered if they were for him. No such luck. One of the Godparents told me they had ignored Aitken and only became animated when the babies arrived. 'Bet it's the first time you've been upstaged by a baby,' he had said to Mr Aitken.

'Give them what they want and they'll go away', Esther said.

She, nanny and I took a baby each and stood in front of the side door.

'Face the front!' shouted the snappers. 'Turn the babies to us.'

'Keep smiling' was Esther's instruction.

The dark interior of the church was illuminated by a succession of bursts of light. It was incongruous and I was incredulous, embarrassed to have been the cause of such a commotion. We walked into the cool, dark quiescence of the building. All eyes turned to us.

I recognized from Bible Class the two other families whose babies were to be baptised and greeted them and those friends I could pick out in the crowd. We walked to the front pew and sat, the babies in their silky robes and hats, each with a bib, just in case. The service began. It was calm and ordered. We sang the hymns, said the prayers and listened while the names of the parents whose children were to be baptised were called out. Two couples and a single name— mine. We walked to the back of the church where the font was. I passed each baby to the vicar. Water was liberally sloshed over each head. None of the babies made a sound. Must have been warmed. Candles were given; certificates were handed out.

A message was whispered to me: 'They're at the side. Best if you get out at the back.' No longer a nice family Christening. It was back to the glare of the media. I left quickly, helped put the babies into the back of the car and we drove out. Photographers ran after the car, flashing through the back window. Those at the gate flashed through the windscreen.

I wondered if there would be press outside the house. Fortunately not. They came later, requesting comment. A guest passed the message down the drive. No comment.

Back to my 150+ guests. Yes, it had been wonderful and the babies had been great. It took us two full days to open all the presents. Such thought had gone into them. Many had 'three' as a theme. My chiropodist had created a silver shape which fitted together into a pattern of three. Three alarm clocks incorporated within three silver cars reflected my own interests. Three books that were so huge the babies could crawl over them and create their own story; one that folded into a play pen with the book round the perimeter. What wonderful friends I had.

A reporter came to the door asking for names. He was polite and well-spoken. Before all this, I would never have dreamed of such an abrupt reaction, but now I said 'I won't talk to you. Please leave.' Another phoned. I said 'It's been a wonderful day and the babies have been great. Now make something of that.'

23

Three Little Brits

That Christmas I received good wishes from the Home Office. These came at the end of a letter rejecting the boys' US birth certificates and requesting the medical evidence leading to their being issued. The 'evidence' was, of course, the mother's say-so. But the Home Office already had the letter from the IVF clinic. Did they assume the IVF clinic was making it up?

The official asked for an immediate response. He got one. I promptly faxed him on New Year's Eve telling him that he already had the evidence. But I also asked whether a DNA test would settle the issue once and for all.

Rather than wait the three months that was becoming the norm for a response, I went ahead and contacted a few agencies. One of them sent out a 'Private and Confidential' letter with 'Paternity Testing' clearly visible under the address in the window envelope.

The one I chose, however, was a branch of the Home Office. It would take 4-6 weeks, but at least there would be proof.

The letter had also said 'We are considering how the Immigration Rules might apply to your case as they can allow the admission of children where it can be established that the surrogate 'parent' is also their biological parent.'

I did not see myself as a quote-unquote 'parent' or, indeed, a 'surrogate' but, if this was the way to get settlement, I would shell out my £600 and have a pin stuck in my finger.

Our GP, splendidly supportive, agreed to carry out the test and the kit was sent to him. He came to our house in early January 2002 armed with plastic containers, envelopes and a wad of forms. Just a jab for me and a swab for each of the boys, I thought. Three hours later, he had completed the last of the forms and enveloped up the samples. The procedure had been so surrounded by safeguards that I was surprised the presence of a neutral observer had not been insisted on.

'What do I owe you?'

The doctor turned his palms skywards. 'How do you quantify this? Have it as a belated Christening present.' It was certainly the most unusual present one could imagine. I accepted with gratitude this very kind gesture.

Six weeks later, on 27 February 2002, the results came back. They made odd reading for one unversed in biochemistry.

They explained if, prior to the DNA evidence, there was believed to be an evens chance of paternity, then the DNA findings would change this to odds of

380,000 to 1 for Piers, 920,000 to 1 for Ian and 43,000 to 1 for Lars. This would result in a probability of paternity of 99.99% for each of the children.

99.99%—enough, I was sure, to send someone to prison for life. I hoped it would be enough for the Home Office. The original of the results was in the post by recorded delivery within an hour of my receiving it.

* * *

I was glad I had gone ahead and undertaken the DNA test.

Three months after my letter of 31 December asking if this would resolve everything, I had still received no reply from the Home Office. Clearly they had no interest in resolving the issue with any speed. For all they cared, I could be kept dangling.

I threw caution aside.

'Indefinite leave to remain' was what I had applied for as a first step. I had sent off the results and was waiting. Nevertheless, 'leave' was permission, not a right. I decided use the 99.99% to apply for Citizenship for the boys. I downloaded the appropriate forms from the internet.

The Citizenship rules could not have been clearer: 'If the child is illegitimate, parent means the mother'. My letter accompanying the application forms and my cheque for £120.00 contained this paragraph: 'If this application is to be rejected on the basis that I am not the parent because I am not the mother of these illegitimate children, please advise by return so I can pursue a case under Article 14 of Human Rights legislation preventing discrimination on the grounds of gender.'

Everything was cc-ed to David Rendel MP. His response was refreshingly unambiguous. 'I, for one, feel it would be utterly absurd were you to be turned down.'

* * *

The really important developments seemed to happen when I was in the kitchen. In the middle of preparations for a chicken chasseur on Tuesday 12 March, Nicky phoned from David Rendel's Office.

'We've been on the phone to the Home Office and they've told us that you'll hear from them in a few days. They've been given indefinite leave to remain.' Just like that.

After the best part of a year, without preamble, the uncertainty was over.

'You might have told me to sit down first.' was my instant reaction. My second was to let a tear trickle. My third was to put a bottle of champagne in the fridge to celebrate with friends.

The first battle had been won. They could stay. I had never doubted it, but now it was Citizenship that I had set my sights on.

I decided I would tell no one until I had given the Citizenship Branch of the Home Office the chance to refuse, grant or, at least, acknowledge. I wrote that day to tell them that the boys had been given indefinite leave to remain and ask again for Citizenship. Surely, they had no option. If the 99.99% is sufficient proof for settlement, it must be sufficient for Citizenship. For the first time I felt the ground become solid.

In May, I was in a shop when my mobile rang. It was David Rendel's secretary telling me the Home Office had granted Citizenship.

I savoured victory for a few moments. My little ones were now as British as could be. Another bottle of Moet went into the fridge and an application for passports into the postbox. These arrived almost by return.

In my heart of hearts, I had known this must happen, known that common sense would prevail, known that this was a precedent that needed to be set. No battles; no doubt. I was now officially a daddy.

But I remained a carer for my father. That aspect of our lives—almost unremarked on by the press for its mundanity, but of huge import to my family—continued without remission.

24

The Greeks Have a Word for It

It's a strange word 'carer'. One is caring. That's good and positive. But the nominalisation into 'carer' is a task, a job, for some a life sentence. It is unrelenting, often unrewarding and can take your life away. I am not sure when I realised that is what I had become. It had crept up on me over the years.

For the first two years of their life, my children saw me physically manoeuvre and sometimes half-carry my father from his bedroom along the landing to the bathroom and steer him back again. I would change him, wash him, shave him and dress him while nanny got the boys ready for the day.

Sometimes, they would hear him sing snatches from 'West Side Story' and 'Carousel'; sometimes hear him telling me to 'bugger off you bastard' with a raised fist.

Over the years, his dependency had become almost total. A few years back I would not have dreamed that I would be wiping his bottom. Now I did not give it a second thought.

There was no embarrassment on his part. He had gone far beyond this point. There was nothing, no matter how intimate, that I was not doing for him. It had simply become my life.

He was always clean and tidy. When he went to day care, his reports testified to how well-presented he was. He had always prided himself on a smart appearance. It was important for me that he looked the part. From a distance, no one would have known there was anything wrong. That is how I would like it to be if anything happened to me.

Some days were better than others, but it was an inevitable decline, not a getting-better-situation. I had to pluck order from chaos, and it was slowly getting worse.

'You're the jam in the sandwich' one of my friends had remarked at that time. I felt like jam—pressed between the insistent demands of the very young and the equally vociferous needs of the very old. There was neither the time nor the energy for any sense of self.

The District Nurse told me that when it was all over, I would not be able to figure out how I managed. She was right. I imagine large amounts of adrenaline were pumping. Each day had to be structured so that I could combine my various roles.

On one particularly bright spring morning, in an instant, I was to realise fully the value of everything I had when I so nearly lost it all. On that day the boys had left early for a trip out with nanny and her friends. I had agreed to this with some reluctance. Nanny had not long passed her driving test. The day had started like any other. I had breakfast with the boys and read to them from 'Thomas the Tank Engine' afterwards.

The planned trip had been presented to me just that morning as a *fait accompli*. Rather than spoil everyone's arrangements, I allowed nanny to take the boys. 'We'll be in convoy, so it'll be safe,' nanny had told me. She fastened the seats into her white Astra and I waved the boys goodbye.

My day with my father was beginning. When I had put him to bed that night, I had turned him to the wall but, as happened most nights, he had slipped backwards onto the mattress that I had left for a soft-landing. By this time, I was sleeping like a cat, alert to the slightest sound. I glanced at the green digits on my clock. It generally happened between two and three. This night the display read 2.22. By using both arms and a leg, I could pivot on the other knee and swivel him back to bed. I made up a story in a quiet voice to reassure him that all was well and sat until I heard rhythmic breathing. By half past three, I was back in bed and knew I would be zonked for the next day. It was becoming the norm. As long as I followed my regular pattern, I knew I would be able to cope.

That day was to be different. I had managed to get my father into the shower when the telephone rang.

I propped him against the wall so he would not fall and ran to answer it. The voice at the end of the line was tremulous; there were children's cries in the background. It was one of the other nannies.

'Ian? Look, there's been an accident.'

I could hear the wail of what the children would thereafter call a 'dee-dah car' in the background.

'There's been an accident. She's turned the car over. The ambulance is on its way.'

The sound of running water reminded me that I had left my father alone. I was to-the-point.

'Anyone dead?'

'No. They're just screaming.'

'I'll call you back.'

Heart pounding, I extricated my father, dried him and sat him on his bed.

'I'll be back in a minute to dress you.'

I dialled 1471 and called back.

'They're OK. Just a few cuts. They're being taken to Winchester Hospital.'

I phoned round to see if someone could sit with my father for the time being. That arranged, heart in mouth, I drove down the A34 as fast as I could.

'I'm so sorry!' Nanny was in floods and the room was filled with the screams of three 15 month-old babies. 'I'm so sorry.'

She was distraught. There was no point in recrimination.

'Well, you hardly meant to do it.'

The doctors had removed Piers' and Ian's clothes and I could see that there were bruises from the seat belts. Nothing more serious. Lars was bleeding from the head. Chunks of glass scrunched onto the floor as each layer of his clothing was removed. The doctor was concerned about internal injuries as he was so distressed. I took his tiny, writhing, howling frame in my arms.

He fell silent. In that instant, for the first time I fully understood what it was to be a parent. Even though I was surrounded by children and adults in tears, blood and glass, the moment was magical.

Thinking about it afterwards, this was the point at which I gained the confidence of knowing that these were *my* children, that they looked to me, that I was their daddy and the most important person in their world. And I knew that I loved them more than I had ever loved anyone.

My eyes met Lars's and filled. I knew I had to be strong, be organised, cope with all the responsibilities. Both he and I knew that he was safe.

This was not the time for tears. I handed Lars back to the doctor.

'Now we can be pretty sure they're just superficial flesh wounds. Glad you're here,' he said.

Back to reality. There were practical issues. I turned to nanny.

'Did you manage to bring the child seats with you? I can't get the children out of here without them'

'No. The police wouldn't let me. They said they it would be dangerous to use them again.'

I knew no shops in Winchester, but assumed that there would be an Argos and that it would have the brand that we had been using. I phoned them and reserved the only three in stock. Rather than negotiate the one-way system, I called a taxi, collected the seats and drove the children home. Later that day, nanny came back with the seats she had removed from what was left of her car. She told me her rear wheel had caught a grass bank on the main A343 road between Andover and Newbury at 60 miles an hour. Out-of-control, the car had skidded across the opposite carriageway. Luckily nothing was coming in that direction. It had hit the bank and turned over. She handed me the remains of the children's seats. One had been broken in half by the impact. The other two were soaked and reeked of petrol. In a parallel universe, I might be alone right now.

Back home, I sat with my three sons and my father aware that none of them had any idea what had happened that day. They were all so precious to me. A moment of carelessness in a car had changed me once and had very nearly done so again.

* * *

There was nothing specific, no warning bells, but I sensed that the fraught way in which I lived was about to change. There were days when I thought 'what have I forgotten?' and then it came to me. I had forgotten to eat. The change came sooner than I had anticipated.

I was on my own on Christmas Day in 2002—or as alone as one can be with three small children and an elderly dementing father to look after. I decided to let him sleep while I dressed the boys, sat them down to breakfast and started opening presents. He had slipped out of bed that night and it had taken a while to get him settled.

He would be tired, so I thought I might be able to get the boys organised and playing in the nursery before attending to him.

My plan was working perfectly. I had cooked the turkey the previous day, so lunch would be as simple as possible while still being the traditional British Christmas dinner.

The boys had no idea what Christmas was about. The rocking horse was too tall for them to clamber onto its saddle and clasp its leather bridle. The bright wrapping paper was of more immediate appeal and we played in the hall amid the clutter while I kept a customary ear cocked for sounds of waking from upstairs.

I managed to feed the children their turkey before my father woke, so I dispensed with his breakfast, deciding to go straight into lunch. Boys safely in the nursery, I manoeuvred my father out of bed and into the bathroom, showered him, shaved him, dressed him and then sat him in the sitting room with Vera Lynn on a CD while I gave the boys a drink. It was at times like these, juggling two surprisingly similar roles, that I amused myself by bringing to mind David Mellor's pithy epithet about me: 'Spoilt millionaire.' Chance would be a fine thing!

When I came down from the children, it was clear that my father was not himself. I moved him to the lavatory. He was leaning to one side. It was his custom to wander around the room, feeling the walls and the door telling me 'Let me out!'

As it was a mild day, so I put his coat on and took him down the drive to look at the garden he had cre-ated. I gave him his tea. Eating had become a problem for him. His food needed to be semi-liquidised, but even this was falling out of his mouth.

After I had put the boys to bed, I carried him up the stairs to his bedroom, feeling the sweat trickling down into small of my back. He was trying to tell me something. 'The Greeks have a word for it,' he said, frustrated but with sudden clarity.

Those were the last words he ever said.

The next morning, Boxing Day, when I carried him to the bathroom, he went deadweight. I put him on the floor. His legs flailed. I called for an ambulance. The paramedics came and helped me put him to bed.

From that moment, he needed to be fed and given fluids. The boys sat with me while I did this. They knew that he was their grandfather and that he was a great man. A few days into 2003 in the early hours of the morning, he died.

I was sleeping on the mattress by his side. It must have been the cessation of his stentorian breathing that woke me. I kissed him, closed his eyes, took my duvet back to my room, made my bed and phoned the doctor.

It had been a physically exhausting and emotionally draining nightmare. I have no idea how I managed. I just got on with it. I was on my own. It was all up to me. I was alone and utterly responsible.

I have long accepted this as a fact. There are no regrets. I did what I had to do, would do it all again and am, indeed, doing just that. The difference is that this time it is a getting-better situation. There is hope, development and growth. All these are denied to the carer.

25

Cuddles

Bringing up three small boys on my own is all about moving on from one point to another. They develop and change and I do so with them. Life is busy, but remarkably normal. I have three sons who depend on me, look to me as an example, who love me and are loved. 'Daddy cuddle! Daddy cuddle!' They bounce up and burrow themselves into me.

Had I not written it down at the time, I would not wish to remember the journey to this point. Against all the odds, I have created both a family and a precedent.

Although all the correspondence and calls I received from the British public and overseas were warm and supportive, I bore in mind the barbed words of those who were not.

I decided to look closely, critically and far too introspectively at possible motivations.

Had I done it to become my mother? Was it that when she died, I had felt as though I had nothing? With children I could assume her role and be to them as she had been to me. If so, I had reckoned without the hormones. My love for them had developed as they had. It had not been absolute from the start.

Had I seen the end of my filial duties approaching? First one parent dies, then the other. Without my role as carer, did I lack a focus to my life? Faced with the great emptiness of freedom, had I decided to exchange one form of servitude with another—that of caring for children?

Both of these hypothesised that I wanted my life to carry on the same way while the storm of change was battering down my accustomed landscape. I would have no mother, but be a mother-figure; I would have no father to care for, but swap him for children.

Was I being too hard on myself?

Or was it that—surrounded by children the horizons of whose vocabulary extended no further than 'wee-wee, potty' and a nanny whose cultural aspirations were fully satisfied by Radio 210—I was indulging myself with imaginative fantasies?

These thick-coming fancies were making me brainsick. I would pluck them out. There were no 'authorities' at my door. They had been conspicuously absent.

No one was judging me. I had been in thrall to this fear from the outset.

I started looking after the boys on my own. It was great to have my life back again.

However accommodating those who helped me had been, while someone else's constant presence was there, neither my home, my life, nor my children felt my own. I needed to be the father I had intended to be when I started on this journey.

It was quite easy to be this by taking control again. Nanny had taught me a great deal. I could not have chosen a better one. I felt confident to take over. It had to come sometime.

* * *

I decided not to have a nanny any longer. She had been away for an operation for an ache which turned out to be a piece of wood embedded in her from the car accident. All this time, the boys did not mention her name. I assumed this meant that my two year-olds were not inextricably attached to her and that this would be the right time to make the change.

We parted amicably. She has visited several times since and taken them out.

On her last day with us there were tears. 'I've managed to do it up to now, but this time I've failed. I've come to love them. I don't think I'll carry on nannying.' (She did, of course, I am glad to say. She had been wonderful.)

The dining area had been upstairs, next to the nursery. I moved their high chairs into the kitchen.

'OK, boys, we having lunch downstairs'. They walked past the alcove without a second glance and into the kitchen they trotted. At this age, they were utterly adaptable.

I decided the boys would benefit from the cut and thrust of nursery; from being with girls and boys their age. They were duly enrolled. From the first day they loved being with other children and I loved getting them ready in the morning and talking to them about 'school' when I collected them.

'What did you do at school today, Lars?'

'Painting.'

'What did you paint?'

'The table and my nose.'

For the first time I felt like a 'normal' parent. They were my children. I was no longer the interloper in the nursery.

'Daddy do it', was the phrase I heard from my sons most often. And daddy was doing it. And he didn't think he was making a bad job of it.

* * *

From then on I knew what it was like to be a father, mother, referee, playmate, cook, cleaner, teacher, driver and factotum sometimes simultaneously, sometimes in succession and often multiplied by three. I realised what a sensible lady Mother Nature is. One at a time, and two to help each other.

Toddlers do not usually come in threes. It is on those rare occasions when I must deal with one or the other on his own that I realise the compromises essential for dealing with three at the same time.

I had assumed chicken pox would strike them all together. No such luck. They were away from school one at a time. Ian caught it, Piers caught it from him and Lars has either not caught it at all or has had it with just one spot.

When each was in the house with me on his own, life slowed to a gentle trot and there was even silence.

Maybe it's only the single parent of triplets who can

say that one baby is easy. When the three are together, they are obsessed with and their lives are dominated by their sense of each other. Lars tosses his pyjamas into the air as I undress him on the changing table. They flutter to the floor.

'Thanks, Lars. Daddy had them all ready to put on you.'

'Piers did it' is the immediate reply.

'I want my... (fill in the blank with whatever toy, book, building brick, crayon, sock, piece of paper a sibling has).'

'Are all the toys yours, Piers?'

'Yes.'

Even bodily functions are a source of rivalry.

'I've done a biiiig pooh.'

'Well done, Ian.'

'It's only tiny,' opines Lars, looking critically into the bowl. 'My pooh was huge.'

The similarities between the elderly dementing and young children are there, too. One never knows quite what to expect and if they are left alone, the unexpected is bound to happen. But they are smaller and the element of random violence is hardly a factor. At least one is unlikely to be belaboured round the head with a full nappy or given a karate chop to the back of the neck while bending to fasten a clean one. My work as a carer has stood me in good stead. It is so far back that I cannot remember a time when I have not had to wipe other people's bottoms.

26

Gashlycrumb Tinies

I knew about children but I had really no idea about toddlers. Much of what I have learned has come from the various remarkable women who helped me in the early years. I now know the importance of continuity, of routine, of as many cuddles as possible, of the constant reassurance that they are loved. I grew into the role as the children grew up.

Nevertheless, nothing, not even the most difficult moments with my father, prepared me for dealing with all the unformed, raw emotions of three small boys who, when they had a mind to, were not averse to taking a chunk out of each other with their teeth.

Ian started it off. Like a mother bird squawking when the hunter comes near the nest, revealing its whereabouts and endangering the contents that are most precious to her, Piers would say 'Ian not do it. Ian not…'

Whatever it was he was not to do, Piers had given the game away. Ian knew just what he had to do to rile his brother and did it.

In the ensuing brouhaha, teeth were bared and I cast around for advice.

I got the same advice from everyone. I was doubtful about it. It couldn't work. They took their cue from their daddy. It was going against all logic. But I was told it worked and that everyone did it. I bided my time.

I was on my back on the floor, playing, lifting Lars up into the air. Piers and Ian were yelling. 'Me! Me!' I saw Ian sink his teeth into Piers's back.

Quick as a flash I was there. Ian knew I had seen him. It was at this point that the collective wisdom I had been given should have cut in. I should have bitten him. I looked Ian in the eye. He may have sensed what was going through my head. Maybe my lips twitched for an instant. He started yelling, feet thumping on the floor. I knew it would be disastrous. For a few minutes, I let the tantrum run its course. Ian's brothers looked on, wondering what daddy would do. Daddy was wondering, too. The little legs stopped and curled. The noise quietened.

'That's not the way to behave, Ian, is it? You shouldn't bite your brother, should you? What would you think if daddy bit you?'

I thought his expression was one of regret.

'So having bitten Piers, what are you going to do now? Bite daddy?'

I extended my hand. Without a second thought, his head was down and his teeth were in.

Tantrums were tricky. I had heard about them, but the concatenation of unfettered emotion that springs from nowhere still took me aback. With three at the same age, squabbles (mainly over toys) were very frequent. Maybe talking through the component parts of a tantrum might help. 'Look boys,' I would say, pointing at the one with the incipient rage, 'Your brother is really angry.' To him, 'Why don't you have a tantrum? Go on, you've got to lie on the floor and bang your fists on the carpet. Yes, and why don't you thump with your feet, too? Oh, really tame. You've got to do it with more spirit and lots of crying and screaming to make it a proper tantrum. That's really weak.'

Slow to learn, I again offered my hand, but at too early a point in the process. It stopped the tantrum, but Lars was so mortified, he was sick all morning.

I suppose sharing is an acquired skill. They enjoyed the stories of 'Leo the Lion' (he who only wanted to love and 'never once asked for a thing') and 'Boo and Blossom' (who cemented their friendship by giving each other whatever was precious to them.) They did not disagree when I told them to give was more blessed than to receive. Putting it into practice was harder. They loved to possess. Often what they loved to possess was the very object of desire that a brother was possessing at that moment.

There are plenty of toys in the world. Most of them live in my sons' nursery. They are surrounded by possessions. Although 'no toys, please' was the request for their third birthday, almost all the 70 plus guests brought three of them. As Ian's Dutch Godmother said, 'It isn't a birthday without presents.'

After the party, we opened some of them. The card was thrown to the floor and the bright wrapping torn asunder. The contents were unboxed, rifled through, dropped, trodden underfoot. Thirty small fingers groped for the next package. Nothing was being valued or appreciated. Small pieces of plastic were being separated from other small related pieces of plastic, never to be reconnected.

Much to their chagrin, I removed the remaining presents to another room. We opened them one at a time over the next month so that each could be savoured before it became an object to be competed for. Even so, several toy boxes, all the bookshelves and most of the wardrobes were taken over by clutter. Piers's cot became so full, he cried because there was no room for him to sleep. In the morning he would be crying because my man; my rabbit; my BarBar; my clown; my piece of plastic that had been separated so long that its original purpose was no longer know-able—had fallen out. Their sheer quantity became a problem he could not cope with. In the belief that less can be more, I bequeathed most of the plethora of toys to ChildLine. Only then did their clear favourites emerge as objects to treasure.

Yet amid the chaos that three tiny children can create for each other and for their parent, there are hilarious moments. Most of these are the non sequiturs and incongruities absent from adult conver-sation. One of the first was, 'I've got tummy ache in my eye.'

Looking out of the streaked nursery window, unable to go out, I said, 'It's pouring down.' 'Yes, it's raining, too', said Lars.

When the children became used to being read sto-ries, Lars would grab the 'brag book' that Tina had sent me full of photographs of them during their first week of life.

'Can you read this one?' he would ask earnestly.

I took the book upstairs.

'Once upon a time there were three small boys. Their names were Piers, Ian and Lars. They lived with their daddy. Although they loved each other very much, they would always squabble. When Piers picked up a toy, Ian and Lars immediately wanted to play with it, too.'

Many is the story that has emanated out of thin air. Later, after I had told them what it contained, his request changed to: 'Read "When We Was Born", please, daddy'.

In their first month at nursery school, I wondered what on earth they were doing including political figures in their songs. 'Alistair Campbell has one hump' came from the back of the car as I drove them home. The next day, not only did he have one hump, but he also had two. The following day, he had three humps as well. I sang it back to them.

'Alistair Campbell has one hump. Alistair Campbell has two humps.'

'No! It's Alistair Campbell!'

'That's what Daddy said!'

It was only when I asked one of the nursery staff, that I was told it was 'Alice the Camel' who had the hump.

When they came home from school, I would say, 'Drink up your milk and then you'll get a chocolate egg.'

'Don't want milk.'

'If you don't drink it, you'll get none.'

Ian looked at me, relieved. Here was something he could get without having to drink milk.

'I want none! I want none!'

When they returned to nursery school having been away with a tummy bug, I told the boss lady at nursery school that their stools were now formed.

'And how are you?' she enquired solicitously.

'Formed, too, thanks' was the automatic reply.

* * *

And there are the moments that are only funny in retrospect. When you are only two, hysterical screaming can be a dropped toy or something of more significance.

'What's the matter with Ian?'

'I think he's yelling because you're shutting his finger in the door.'

The young nursery assistant was distraught. One of her colleagues plunged the throbbing finger into cold water.

'Never mind, you didn't mean it.'

After a wakeful night, I told their favourite teacher that Ian has been up much of the night because his little finger still hurt from being caught in the door

'Oh, which one is that?' she asked absently.

'The one that's red, swollen and painful. The one he's waving about.'

While I was thinking about all the various titles a parent has, I realised I had lost mine. I no longer had my name. Having called myself 'daddy' to the children, I found myself using this name first to the cats, then to myself and, eventually, occasionally to grown-ups in general conversation. I taught the boys their second names and they proudly stressed them.

'I'm Piers *Thomas* Mucklejohn.'

'Who are you, Ian?'

'Ian *Aidan* Mucklejohn.'

'And. Lars, who are you?'

'I'm Lars *Conrad* Mucklejohn.'

'And,' pointing to myself, 'who's this?'

The response was instant.

'Daddy Mucklejohn.'

'Doesn't daddy have another name?'

Again instantly.

'Mucklejohn.'

I thought I wouldn't complicate matters. My sons had no idea what my name was. I would be 'Daddy Mucklejohn' for the foreseeable future. When I answered the phone: 'Ian Mucklejohn', Lars piped up to correct me, 'Ian's sitting at the table.'

Long-held assumptions disappeared as well. On the day they were born, down went their names on the list of a nice private prep school some miles away in the countryside. I had not dared tempt providence by doing it earlier.

The application form asked which public school they would be going to. A tiny warning bell rang. I had no idea what my children would be like, so how could I answer that question? It was to be a few years before I listened properly to that bell. Did I really want these three little boys of mine to have friends scattered across the south of England? They should have friends in the houses near where we live.

I visited all the local infant schools. Their grounds did not extend as far as the eye could see and the classes were certainly larger, but all the uniformed children were purposefully engaged in one activity or another, the staff had superb control and the head teachers were clearly committed. I was impressed. This was the local community. This was what I wanted my sons to be part of, not the cocooned, rarefied environment of a small world to which I had become accustomed, inhabited by alice bands, their intimidating four-wheel drives disgorging Hugos to relate with identical Hugos and, in the fullness of time, to create their own Hugos.

I wanted them to feel an affinity with their town, not a company, however charitable; however limited by guarantee.

I recalled yet another lesson I had learned from Dutch parents. 'Here,' I was told, 'only those who are really bad or have something wrong with them go to private schools. Everyone goes to state schools. That's why they're good. If there is something wrong with the school, parents act to change it; to make it better. In the UK, if you don't like what the state school provides and if you've got the money, you just take your child away and go private. The effect is that intelligent and articulate parents keep the Dutch state schools on their toes. In the UK, they opt out.'

After so many years connected with private schools in one way or another, I had overlooked how divisive they could be. I was lucky to have such good state schools locally and no competing secondary private school to cream off those talented youngsters whose parents could pay the bill. I decided I would be proud to have my children in the state system and encourage them to contribute to its excellence.

I could hardly believe how having children was making me look at life in such a new way. I thought I knew all the answers. Now I understand that I had no idea what the questions were. Time will tell as to the permanence of this particular perspective.

When I had been a fully-functioning parent for a while and had more than a passing idea what it entailed, I found myself sensitive to perceived snubs.

While no one made any critical comments to my face, a friend told me what her mother had said when she told her she was going to visit us. 'Oh, has he still got them then?' That the statement that had precipitated the question had contained the answer within it made me wonder why it had been asked—and why it had been asked with such casual indifference.

Had she not been in her nineties, my father's sister's comments would have stung, too. With failing sight, widowed and childless, living on the other side of London, my father had remained in telephone contact with her. In the later years, she told me it distressed her too much to hear his voice, so I kept her informed of his well-being and told her about the children. One call coincided with a piece in the *Daily Mail*.

'The neighbours told me they've seen you in the press again dragging the family name through the mud. But you never really were one of the family were you? Your mother saw to that, taking you off to the country.'

That had been a long time brewing.

'I suppose you won't want to phone me again.'

'I'll keep you posted about my father.'

I took him to see her, but she asked me not to bring him back. After his death, I took the boys to see her and she phoned me afterwards to say how sweet they were. When she died in 2004, there were only two relatives—a niece and a nephew—my cousin and me. My cousin inherited half a million pounds worth of house and contents. I was left a wooden door stop in the shape of a piece of cheese topped by a mouse that little Ian had enjoyed playing with.

My father would have been shaken. My mother would have considered her true-to-form.

* * *

Children pick up quickly on parental quirks and adopt them as their own. With my own background as an English graduate, it came as second nature to introduce my children to poetry at an early stage. I went straight into assonance, alliteration and metre. Out came the more than slightly foxed copy of the 1939 *Oxford Book of English Verse* that my father had read to me as a child and from whence came my own love of words.

For most children, 'Q' is for 'Queen', but for the boys, 'Q' is for 'Quinquireme'. My arm swung gently as if holding an oar as I read 'Quinquireme of Nineveh from distant Ophir, Rowing home to haven in sunny Palestine, With a cargo of ivory, And apes and peacocks, Sandalwood, cedarwood, and sweet white wine.'

They were captivated by the rich, full vowels and sibilants; words that brought on salivation by their very voluptuousness. My hand made soft round movements to simulate rippling waves as I continued,

'Stately Spanish galleon coming from the Isthmus, Dipping through the Tropics by the palm-green shores, With a cargo of diamonds, Emeralds, amethysts, Topazes, and cinnamon, and—pausing to let the richness of the sounds take effect—gold moidores.'

Their eyes widened. Then the tempo raced with staccato syllables spitting out at speed. The boys giggled and clapped their hands in surprise and delight at the change. 'Dirty British coaster with a salt-caked smoke stack, Butting through the Channel in the mad March days, With a cargo of Tyne coal, Road-rails, pig-lead, Firewood, iron-ware, and cheap tin trays.' By the end, they were laughing out of control. 'Read 'Queen of Nivea'!' is the constant refrain at bedtime.

John Masefield's 'Cargoes' would pave the way for other linguistic delights. One reading of Edward Gorey's *Gashlycrumb Tinies* was enough to consign the large, colourful book that began 'A is for Apple' to the back of the cupboard. For the boys 'A is for Amy, who fell down the stairs; B is for Basil, assaulted by bears; C is for Clara, who wasted away; D is for Desmond, thrown out of a sleigh'.

27

How Do You Manage

'How on earth do you manage?' is a question often put to me. Looking after three children alone and without any family support is a tall order. Although the primal parent is certainly present and my barometric inner ear can sense the change in pressure from the tiniest cry of distress at night, when I relinquished nanny and went solo, I knew it would only work with organisation.

The priority was to get the children on side. As nanny had been strict to the point of firmness, this was made easy for me. I think the trick was to make everything their achievement rather than mine. Their nursery has floor-to-ceiling wardrobe mirrors along a wall. It was covered with hand prints. 'Look boys, this is a mess, isn't it? Daddy has to clean it, you know. You'll be able to see yourselves better without fingermarks, won't you?' Only a couple of reminders were needed. 'Gosh, these mirrors look great. What a clean nursery you have!' They love the mirrors. Even during the most intense daddy-cuddle, I catch them looking at themselves.

But amazingly I have never seen even the slightest mark of a finger on them again. 'And not on the car either, please.' Sure, enough, their little fingers did not touch the windows there. 'And not the walls on the corridor.' Again. No problem. They self-corrected. If their little fingers strayed, they would remind themselves out loud.

To say that I owe it all to my mother may be trite, but it is true. The more I am with the boys, the more the memories flood back. I am doing what she did; what she would have done. I catch myself using her words.

Perceptively, someone had asked me if I knew who the boys' mother was. My response was that I knew who their grandmother was.

I am talking to them as my mother talked to me. From the earliest days she taught me to value everyone for who that person is.

I have an early and vivid memory of being in London when I was about three. I was on a bus with her. She took my hand and drew me to her. 'You're going to see something you haven't seen before. There's nothing to be frightened of.' The bus pulled in at a bus stop. She had seen the queue of people. As he put his hand on the rail and pulled himself in, I gasped and pressed into my mother, terrified. This was the first black man I had seen. That was 1950. At the time, we started the day at Primary School with a hymn, the first verse of which started in a low, confidential tone:

Over the sea there are little brown children

Fathers and mothers and babies dear.'
(Up an octave and rising to a pleading crescendo)
'They do not know there's a Father in Heaven
No one has told them that Christ is near.'
(Then with a smug assurance that all would be well)
'Swift let the message go over the water
Telling the children that Christ is near.

How different it is in today's multicultural Britain. 'There's a man running.' The boys had seen him through the car window. 'Yes,' I said. 'He a…' I paused and rejected the qualifier. 'A man—running.' The child in their nursery group whose name I don't know is the girl with the pale blue top and dark hair, not the Chinese girl.

At my primary school, all the families were the *Mail*'s ideal. There were no single parents and no divorces or separations. Whether these were happy nuclear families was a question never asked. Relationships were not spoken of.

Fifty years later my children's friends' parents speak openly of their emotions, sometimes in front of their children. Family structures are a reflection of a seismic social shift. Many parents are single; several are splitting painfully; some are openly critical of each other; one family takes holidays together—cuckold, lover and all.

'You're the ones who should be on the 'Trisha' programme', I remarked. 'You're far more interesting than I am.'

* * *

Even in such a short time, I can see how different my children's lives are from my own. I would be walked to nursery school. We had no car. Most people had no car. When we did have one, it was a pre-war banger. I would listen to the wireless. We had no TV. Hardly anyone had one. It was a special treat to go down the road to view the Coronation in 1953. The doors of an ornate wooden console were opened to reveal a small, curved screen on which, when it had warmed up, appeared a fuzzy black-and-white image of Her Majesty. Now, as new houses stand in the way of a short-cut to a five-minute walk to nursery school, they ride in a car while listening to CDs and at home they watch DVDs.

I had no idea of foreign countries or their languages at their age. Through my work, they meet people from all over the world and know that they use other tongues. As a child I was aware of Germany and the influence of the war on my family's life. The family home had been hit during the Blitz. My uncle, who had been cleaning his bicycle, was sucked out and had been found up a tree, alive and still clinging to his bike. Everything else had been lost except the numbers on the front door—22—which adorn the garden shed to this day.

Perhaps it is from this that I became interested in Germany and the German language. All parents, consciously or otherwise, pass on their interests to their children. I did so quite consciously.

'It's an aeroplane', the boys would say every few minutes when we were in the garden. They picked up the faint drone of planes in transit between Heathrow and rest of the world and scoured the skies to find the source. 'Yes, it's an aeroplane,' I would repeat with some tedium.

Then I thought, why not try it in a different language? Children love playing with words and sounds. So 'it's a plane' also became 'it's a Flugzeug' and, carrying on the idea of 'zeug', a toy became a 'Spielzeug' too.

Planes weren't the only objects in the sky. Soon the boys were as likely to come out with 'it's a Hubschrauber' as 'it's a helicopter'.

I tried to match the languages to those their Godparents speak. They loved the funny accents, too. Lars was able to ride in daddy's 'bil' and look at a passing 'tog'. 'What's 'butter' in Norwegian, Lars?' 'Smør' he would reply with a perfect lilt. 'And how about your 'pocket'—what's that?' 'Lomme.' Ian adored travelling along the 'Autobahn' and Piers would greet me with 'Bonjour'. As they came into contact with all my students from round the world at the weekend, they were well aware of words and accents. 'What's 'hello' in French, Ian?' He lowered his head and in a gutteral voice said 'Alo.'

Yet the boys seemed to have a special affinity with German and Germans, just like their father. A thirteen year-old became a great friend of theirs during one summer Course. 'Gib mir fünf', they would say, echoing him, raising their hands to a 'high five' greeting. Their favourite viewing has become the BBC's 'Muzzy' in German. It should be French to prepare them for what will, no doubt, be the main second language at 'big school', but I have far more to do with

Germany than France.

'Do you want 'Kipper'?' I would ask.

'We want 'Mutzi'!' was their reply with perfect German intonation.

'No, don't turn it off! No!' they would say when lunch was ready.

* * *

Some old habits die hard. I find it surprising when the boys mention adults at the nursery by their first name with no honorific prefix. I invariably refer to their Godparents as Auntie and Uncle. Lars' godmother Esther told them, 'The whole world calls me Esther. Even my own children call me Esther. Your daddy's the only one who calls me Auntie Esther. You have full permission to call me Esther boys.' The Godparents are our family.

They are the Aunties and Uncles my sons do not have in a familial sense. They are people who are and will be special to them. They will give them their own special qualities. Realising that I have come to parent-hood late in life, they are also those will take over as executors should I die before my sons are of age.

Having my own children has made me value those of my mother's and father's sisters—cousins, blood relatives. There is a large extended family of which the boys are a part. We now have reunions a couple of times a year. The boys come with me and are much cuddled. 'You look so well on it' was one cousin's comment. 'You were made for this' was another's.

Bicker though they do, the boys' love for each

other, too, is absolute. When Ian had to go into hospital for a tonsilectomy and adenoidectomy, I took his brothers to visit him so they knew where he was. All seemed normal until I brought them back. Lars was sick after each meal until Ian came home. He missed him so much.

As I mediate between Piers, quietly putting the jigsaw together and Ian casting the pieces into the air with Lars providing a running commentary, I find it diverting to reminisce.

My initial instincts had been right—and wrong. Wrong in that I had assumed babies would be on the parent's side and co-operate in being nurtured and provided for. Babies are tricky. They have their own agenda. But I was fundamentally right in thinking that I could do the job. The hurdle I found most difficult to overcome was that put in front of me by the QC.

I had come to believe that there must be a woman involved at all times, that is to say that I *had* to relegate responsibility for their own good. The subconscious thought that, if I had the temerity to manage on my own, some authority would come along and take them away had sunk deep. I automatically ensured as often as possible that there would not be the slightest chance of this.

I advertised for weekend help and went through a succession of more-or-less reliable and worthy staff before I realised that, not only were the authorities not remotely interested in me or my family, let alone plotting to take the children away, but that I was perfectly capable of bringing them up. This realisation came to me slowly, but I was helped towards it by one of the less-than-reliable weekend help who blithely asked me:

'If you had decided to abort one of them, which one would you have chosen?' She it was who had told me: 'There's nothing difficult about looking after babies. They're the same as animals.'

Where I had been absolutely right all along was in knowing that I could do the job. I would never have experienced so many deliciously life-changing moments and three lovely children would never have existed. I am certain every parent feels like this. But what with hindsight I fail to see is why British law-makers put so many obstacles in the way of those who want to have a family?

What are they afraid of? The western world needs more children and there are people with hearts break-ing with love who want so much to be parents. I was lucky. I could do it all privately. The route to parent-hood actually turned out to be a straight road. But along it, chicanes had been placed to slow the traffic.

There is science with its amazing possibilities and here we are, free, but struggling with our self-imposed restrictions. I took advantage of the freedom the US offers. Had I met the doom merchants and self-right-eously religious pro-lifers before making the decision, perhaps I would not have gone ahead. I would have eschewed freedom, viewed it with suspicious caution, sidestepped it, felt that, as here was something that could be abused, it should not be entertained. But there again, anything can be abused and there are plenty of those who will seek to outlaw whatever might fall into that category.

Human nature—as evidenced by the letters I received—is, I believe, fundamentally good and decent. Having done what I did is hardly going to open the floodgates of hoards keen to become single fathers. Very few would wish to. And those who do wish to will have put into the decision as much thought as I did and go ahead only in the knowledge that they would do their utmost to make it succeed. That's all a parent can do. Those who make a conscious decision to achieve parenthood will go through agonies analysing how best to do it.

It may not make them better parents than those who do it accidentally, but it is in no way a disqualification. I found what I thought I would find—prohibitive legislation; restrictions based on the fear of what human beings might do. The joy of what they can achieve given the freedom to do so is boundless. J.-J. Rousseau was quite right. 'Man is born free, but shackled everywhere.'

Maybe fear of litigation will stop the route I took in the fullness of time, but the scope offered by a turn-of-the-century free-thinking American society and state-of-the-art technology has created a new British family with shoots that will reach well into the new millennium.

* * *

I realise how extraordinarily lucky I was. 'You got away with it,' our GP said. 'Multiple births are very risky.'

Had I realised all the complications, I would not

have sanctioned the implantation of four embryos. Triplets are hard work. Nevertheless, I am glad I did not know all this when I started as I would not be without any of my sons for the world. Now that those fuzzy specks have become real people with diverse characters and personalities, I look at the earliest photograph of the boys which must be as early as any family photograph can be and wonder which is which. I also wonder about the one that never made it. The one *who* never made it. And I see in my mind's eye a fourth variation on a theme that was somehow subsumed into the other three. And I feel a loss.

What about the frozen embryos? Those four little incipient life-forms sitting in a Californian freezer. What should I do with them? I used to think that any form of medical research on embryos was grisly.

My belief that life begins at day one is also one of the pro-lifers' tenets, but now that I have personal experience of their capacity to inflict pain through doctrinaire adherence to fundamentalist beliefs, I can see this as another dogma.

An embryo has life. So has a sperm. There is no certainty that an embryo will become a life as we know it but, through the medium of stem-cell research, there is the real possibility that it may save life. I cannot see the difference between the time limits and criteria for abortion and the use of embryos for stem cell research. I can see that the relief of suffering and the improvement of quality of life are noble aspirations and part of what make us human. In time it may well be that such research can cure the sort of illness that blighted my family.

Nevertheless, in my mind's eye I can see four little copies of my three waiting to be brought into existence. I need time for my thoughts to adjust to the idea of using these embryos to advance what I see as a laudable aim.

In fact, my first thought was to give them to 'Snowflakes', an organisation in Los Angeles that donates spare embryos to infertile couples. But if I were to donate them, how would my sons react to the idea that they have siblings out there? Would they make it their life's work to track them down? Would they think that I had simply given their brothers and sisters away?

There is no use-by date on the embryos. I have time—maybe even enough time to ask my sons much later how they might feel about a donation. Or perhaps I should leave the embryos where they are in case my sons' wives have difficulty conceiving. They could have these little fellows implanted and father their own brothers or sisters. Whatever next?

Deciding to remain undecided brings its own relief.

28

'Mummy'

'Where's my mummy?'

Out-of-the-blue one morning, Lars wiped away the foam of toothpaste and asked it again, as if by rote. Not inquisitorial, just a sing-songy question along the lines of the previous one—'Is my toothbrush red?'

It was a question I had been expecting. That it came from the mouth of a three and three-quarter-year-old not yet able to brush his own teeth is what took me by surprise.

'Which one?'

The answer was instinctive. I visualised one of his mothers. I decided on Melissa. It was less complicated to answer about her. 'I don't really know, Lars. I think she's in America.'

There was a slight pause while Lars took the offered mug, swished water round his mouth and spat it out, twice.

'Can I see her?'

'Not yet, no.' I could see the inevitable 'why?' forming on his lips and anticipated it. 'She's never met you,

Lars, and daddy doesn't know her. I'm afraid you've only got daddy.' Quite what a three and three-quarter year-old child might make of this and how much of it was more than just the repetitive asking of one of his many questions, I had no idea, but had the vague feeling that I should dissipate the notion of rejection before it formed.

'Look, Lars, if she knew you, I'm sure she'd love you very much and want to see you, but she doesn't know you.' The 'and fortunately hasn't expressed the slightest interest in getting to know you' hung in my head.

'Is America in Newbury?'

'Much further away than that.'

'Is it the other side of Newbury?'

'Lars, we're not going to see her.'

'Can we go and see my mummy in America tomorrow?'

'No, Lars, we can't.'

'Can I wipe the basin instead?'

'Yes, Lars. That would be kind.'

He busied himself with a towel. The idea had caught his imagination and he wasn't about to let it go.

'When can I see my mummy in America?'

'Lars, I don't know.'

'She's got a red car.'

'What sort of red car?'

'Like yours, but it's red. And she's got red and blue shoes and she's got a boat in the bath. It's a black one.'

'Do you know her name?'

'Yes. It's 'Pandora' and she's very small.'

'And is she also a cat?'

'No, don't be a silly daddy. She's a girl. Can I have a daddy-cuddle on the sofa?

He pressed his small frame into my chest, hands clasped round my neck.

'I love you daddy.'

'I love you, too, Lars. Won't daddy do?'

His wiry red hair rubbed against my cheek as he nodded his agreement.

In the meantime, Piers had been demanding the return of his Bob The Builder sketch pad. Rather than be a constant referee, I had decided to make objects that caused squabbles temporarily disappear. The pad had been banished to a high shelf after he and Ian had squabbled over it and the one had brought it down on the head of the other as a way of settling their difference.

'I want it NOW!' Piers had put on his tough-guy expression, corners turned down, nose running, face flushed. 'Or…' His eyes skittered around as he lunged for a verbal weapon. 'Or I'll tell my mummy in America.'

* * *

Maybe the time will come when they will tell their friends that they have two mummies.

Be that as it may, they effectively have none. This is certainly something that parts of the media have berated me for. I have been accused of undervaluing and rejecting women. Not so. I know what it's like to love and be loved; to feel desire; to long for the unique fulfilment that is commitment. I know what a loving relationship means physically and spiritually. I know the sublimation of one soul into another. As happens with many people, whatever might have been did, in the end, not happen—did not work out. It could have happened. My fault that it did not. I should have valued that special someone more. I should not have let the chance of happiness slip through my fingers in my search for the ideal, the perfection that does not and cannot exist. The thought is too painful, however. Nature's safety valve removes from my mind those regrets, strips away the 'if only', excises what cannot be brought back.

For those who are fortunate the special union is achieved. And I know that it is very special and precious. They are blessed. There are no absolutes. We all know instinctively what feels right for us at a certain time. Those of us who, for the myriad of different reasons that are part of the complexity of life and how we live it, do not achieve a lasting relationship, have traditionally had to accept various compromises. In this, as in so many aspects of life, scientific advance has gone hand in hand with more relaxed social attitudes.

Not long ago, what I did could simply not be done. Now it can. That it can be done has been accepted. It cannot be uninvented. That it is something that can positively be embraced will take longer. Not to have formed a lasting relationship used to be a failing. Maybe it is. I see it as something that can happen. It certainly happens with carers. It does not mean that one is less human; less loving; less giving of oneself. It does not mean that one has to resign oneself to lovelessness—or childlessness. It should not mean that one has to run the gauntlet of the tabloid press. Who is so imbued with sanctity or embedded in conventionality to condemn those who find alternative routes to happiness? As I have.

I hope there may be a woman with whom to share this joy in a loving and permanent relationship. Indeed, my children are such a joy, they should be shared. If this happens, I shall have done things in reverse order. If it does not happen, I shall still have the unutterable pleasure of my sons and they will have the certainty of my love. Love, no matter where it comes from, is what is important.

My children are in the position of the many children from single-parent families. On the positive side, they are not party to the acrimony that can follow divorce. They do not experience adult disharmony. I am not sure what the negative side will be. As they are such different personalities, I suspect that there will be no easy answer to this, but as long as I remain able to relate to each of these different people on all manner of different levels, I do not see a significant downside. Time will tell. Like all parents, I am still learning.

What time has taught me is to see life Before Children as BC. I am now in the AD of my life. Everything changes and I have changed with it. For instance, I assumed that people who lived down long drives did so because they didn't want neighbours. I knew other people in the road only by their cars.

It's different now. Whenever we go for a walk, the boys ask if they can visit neighbours. Sometimes it is Cleo the dachshund; sometimes Auntie Vivienne or

Auntie Susan. There are many others. We are always made so welcome. Without the children, I would never have dropped in; never have presumed. The children have no such inhibitions and have given me confidence bordering on effrontery. Now I am really happy to pay unannounced visits and our neighbours are happy to receive them. I know that if ever I were laid so low that I could not cope, I would have no end of help.

And that is one factor I had not even thought about. Illness. BC, I was never ill. Until immunity sets in, I now come down with everything they bring back from nursery school. I can lay awake at night, ravaged by one of the array of viruses that travel between school and home, wondering how on earth I am going to get them up and ready in the morning. As all parents know, you simply cannot be ill.

And they are ill. 'I've hurt my leg, daddy!' I'm not sure if a quick rub with pretend magic spray, a kiss and cuddle and then 'never mind, darling—you've got another one' is the best way to treat these passing disasters. I must try to do better. The most elaborate plans, including the time set aside for writing this book, are thrown into chaos by a single spot or a loose stool. 'I've got earache. Quick! The poo's coming!'

'It's 'diarrhoea', darling.'

'Quick, the dire earache's coming!'

One of them can be laid low for days while the others are rudely healthy. The answer to 'Can we go for a ride on Thomas the Tank Engine?' is sometimes, sadly, 'Piers/Ian/Lars is poorly. We'll have to wait 'til he's better.' They seem to be ill one after the other rather than getting it over and done with in one go. Should I be more sympathetic? Is this the feminine side that may be deficient? Or is this just the soul-searching that is part of every parent's psyche? To be sensitive to the subtle nuances of three small personalities simultaneously requires a combination of psychological skills and saintly virtues that I fear fall short in me. But I try.

'You unset me.'

'I unsettle you? I unseated you? I trod on you?' The corners of the mouth turned down; lower lip extended ready to howl. 'Ah. I upset you! Oh. Sorry, Lars, how did daddy do that?'

'You told me I wasn't being helpful.'

Lars became inordinately sad at any imagined slight. He felt he was a special support to daddy.

'But you did pull the bathrobe off the towel rail when daddy was busy with Piers.'

'I folded it up again!' he sobbed.

The bundle of cloth that daddy had instinctively pulled off the rail and re-folded was the attempt to help that had not been appreciated enough. Must do better next time. I turned to Ian and lifted him into his Grobag.

'Naaaawh. Baby's there!'

His bald doll had been laid under the Grobag.

'With the wheatie.'

'An Apricot Wheatie that you have for breakfast, Ian?'

'No,' was his patient reply. 'Not a 'wheatie'. A 'sweetie'.' Ian had become used to having to say the same thing several times to the point at which he was using quite a variety of different words to describe the same thing. Shades of my past. As the speech therapist he used to see told me: 'All children make some sound substitutions, but Ian makes all the sound substitutions.'

'A sweetie?' I ventured.

'No. The thingy that you put on a high shelf yesterday.'

Everything in the past was 'yesterday'. I remembered the blue plush-covered box that had caused a ruckus the week before.

'Ah! The squeaker!'

'Yesss!' Ian was proud of his newly-acquired sibilant.

The blue box was by baby's side. I zipped Ian up and smoothed the fabric over the doll and the squeaker. He smiled and settled for a few seconds before ejecting the doll from the cot. 'Don't want baby. Want my nuther toy.' At least that was more successful. How about Piers?

'I've got dire earache, daddy.'

'OK, darling. Let's unzip you and pop you on the lavatory.'

He sat bemused, Grobag off and pyjama bottoms round his ankles.

'But I just need some cotton wool in my ear, daddy.'

* * *

I used to think I knew what I was doing; used to cover all my bases. Not any longer. Now there are four of us—and they are not all little versions of me. I am not

the me I was. Nothing is for sure. Three other characters are developing in front of me and all are clam-
ouring to be taken into consideration at the same time.

Relating to each of them one-to-one without
another impinging is hard to arrange. This tends to
happen at cuddling time before bed when those not
being cuddled are playing with toys. It seems to work.
The logistics of how to arrange it in any other way
escape me. I wonder how other parents manage.

I can see that they are far from being the tragic
motherless infants that some sections of the media
have accused me of creating. I never thought they
would be. If I needed any external verification, their
nursery school tells me they are perfectly well-adjust-
ed and happy. 'It makes my day when they come in,'
one of the staff there told me.

Challenging it is, yet even so I feel a confidence different from anything I have felt before. I know that I
can be what these little ones need me to be. And I
know it not just because I must be their guide and protector. It's what I want to be. It is my being.

My experience is only with three. Whenever I have
been with just one of them, generally when that one
is ill, I see the difference. The relationship is easier;
more fluid; without the tensions that rivalry engenders
and the restrictions that impartiality demands. I can be
reflective, empathetic; need to plan less; can have a
spontaneity that three small children and only two
hands precludes. I had never really considered that
there would be more than one child. 'Just the one,
then?' I say when I hear that a friend is expecting. 'A
cinch.' In comparison, it is. A child is hard work. The

load with three is increased exponentially. Now that I know what it's like, I am filled with admiration at the work parents do and have the greatest respect for single mothers—and fathers.

All through this journey, the children—my own and the many others I have come to know—have been great. It is with some of the adults that I have issues that I find hard to resolve. While they were taking pot shots at me, I wonder if the media hacks had any idea of the hurt I felt. Now it would be my children who would share that hurt. Would that adults had the openness and straightforwardness of children.

Now that we are four, I find I have to try to explain away adult behaviour. In this I am quite unsuccessful as I cannot fathom much of it myself. I had not bothered with it before but, with a family, values and attitudes assume greater significance.

How can I explain away their best friend who disappeared from nursery school one day with no goodbye and no further contact from his parents?

Or my old friend whose dog and family my children visited at the seaside and who took his life a few days later?

Seeing the world from a child's point-of-view has made me more questioning; less accepting. I look at the children and think: 'What a world have I brought you into?' The mix of optimism and horror that is history remains. I had never seen it in juxtaposition to a tiny, innocent baby.

In this context, the colours are more vivid. The black is darker. Now my instinctive perspective is that of a vulnerable child who will, in the fullness of time be left with a legacy of challenges from melting gla-ciers to drug-resistant pandemics.

When I watched the events of 9/11 unfold, I squeezed their hands. I brought out my camcorder and filmed them with the TV in the background. 'This will change the world for the next fifty years or more' my commentary runs. Later, I would think of the attack on Pearl Harbour that served to 'awaken a sleeping giant and fill him with a terrible resolve.'

It is not easy to make out a case for the essential goodness that is, I believe, human nature. I have to help my children pick through the morass of misun-derstanding in which we live. The mirror that is a new parent's eye may be a distorting one. Its reflections are nurture, protection, security. I see all these threatened. The grotesque events that have unravelled post September 2001 have made the world so unsafe, have given free rein to such excesses of behaviour on all sides that I know that now, I would never, absolutely never, do it again.

But looking at my three sons today, I am delighted that I did…